Suddenly Last Summer and Other Plays

Tennessee Williams was one of the most influential American playwrights of the twentieth century. Born Thomas Lanier Williams III in 1911 in Columbus, Mississippi, he later changed his name to 'Tennessee' after the state of his father's birth. Williams was diagnosed with diphtheria at the age of seven, causing him to spend much of his adolescence at home. Tennessee's older sister, Rose, suffered from schizophrenia and later underwent a prefrontal lobotomy, after which she was incapacitated. In 1938, Williams entered the University of Iowa and completed his course, at the same time holding down a large number of part-time jobs. Writing continually during this period, Williams soon made his name as a playwright, producing shows in Boston and on Broadway in New York. Whilst living in New Orleans Williams met Frank Merlo, with whom he had a long-term relationship until Frank's premature death in 1961. Tennessee Williams died at his New York City residence, the Hotel Elysee, in 1983.

In 1940 Williams received the Rockefeller Fellowship for his play *Battle of Angels* (later rewritten as *Orpheus Descending*), and with *The Glass Menagerie* in 1944, won the New York Drama Critics' Circle Award, which established him as an important playwright. He won the Pulitzer Prize twice: in 1948 for *A Streetcar Named Desire*; and in 1955 for *Cat on a Hot Tin Roof*. His plays have enjoyed great success both on stage and on screen, some memorable productions of which starred actors Marlon Brando, Vivien Leigh, Katharine Hepburn, Elizabeth Taylor and Paul Newman. Among his many plays Penguin publishes *The Glass Menagerie* (1944), *A Streetcar Named Desire* (1947), *Summer and Smoke* (1948), *The Rose Tattoo* (1951), *Cat on a Hot Tin Roof* (1955), *Baby Doll* (1957), *Something Unspoken* (1958), *Suddenly Last Summer* (1958), *Sweet Bird of Youth* (1959), *Period of Adjustment* (1960), *The Night of the Iguana* (1961), *The Milk Train Doesn't Stop Here Anymore* (1963; revised 1964) and *Small Craft Warnings* (1972). Penguin also publishes Tennessee Williams's *Memoirs*.

Peter Shaffer has written of Tennessee Williams: 'He was a born dramatist as few are ever born. Whatever he put on paper, superb or superfluous, glorious or gaudy, could not fail to be electrifyingly actable. He could not write a dull scene . . . Tennessee Williams will live as long as drama itself.'

T0354180

TENNESSEE WILLIAMS

Suddenly Last Summer

*The Milk Train Doesn't Stop
Here Anymore*

Small Craft Warnings

PENGUIN BOOKS

PENGUIN CLASSICS

Published by the Penguin Group
Penguin Books Ltd, 80 Strand, London WC2R 0RL, England
Penguin Group (USA) Inc., 375 Hudson Street, New York, New York 10014, USA
Penguin Group (Canada), 90 Eglinton Avenue East, Suite 700, Toronto, Ontario, Canada M4P 2Y3
(a division of Pearson Penguin Canada Inc.)
Penguin Ireland, 25 St Stephen's Green, Dublin 2, Ireland (a division of Penguin Books Ltd)
Penguin Group (Australia), 250 Camberwell Road, Camberwell, Victoria 3124, Australia
(a division of Pearson Australia Group Pty Ltd)
Penguin Books India Pvt Ltd, 11 Community Centre, Panchsheel Park, New Delhi – 110 017, India
Penguin Group (NZ), 67 Apollo Drive, Rosedale, North Shore 0632, New Zealand
(a division of Pearson New Zealand Ltd)
Penguin Books (South Africa) (Pty) Ltd, 24 Sturdee Avenue, Rosebank,
Johannesburg 2196, South Africa

Penguin Books Ltd, Registered Offices: 80 Strand, London WC2R 0RL, England

www.penguin.com

020

Suddenly Last Summer first published 1958
Published in this collection in Penguin Classics 2009
Copyright © Tennessee Williams, 1956

The Milk Train Doesn't Stop Here Anymore first published in Great Britain by
Martin Secker & Warburg Ltd 1964
Published in this collection in Penguin Classics 2009
Copyright © Two Rivers enterprises Inc., 1963, 1964

Small Craft Warnings first published in Great Britain by Martin Secker & Warburg Ltd 1973
Published in this collection in Penguin Classics 2009
Copyright © Tennessee Williams, 1970, 1972, 1973
All rights reserved

The moral right of the author has been asserted

Set in Dante MT 10.5/13pt
Typeset by Palimpsest Book Production Limited, Grangemouth, Stirlingshire
Printed in England by Clays Ltd, Elcograf S.p.A.

Professionals and amateurs are hereby warned that these plays are fully protected under the copyright
laws of the United States of America, the British Commonwealth, including the Dominion of Canada,
and all other countries of the world, subject to royalty. All rights, including professional, amateur, motion
pictures, recitation, lecturing, public reading, radio broadcasting, television, and the rights of translation
into foreign languages, are strictly reserved. Applications for amateur performance should be made to
Samuel French Ltd., 52 Fitzroy St., London W1T 5JR. All other enquiries to Casarotto Ramsay & Associates
Ltd., 7–12 Noel St., London W1F 8GQ

Except in the United States of America, this book is sold subject
to the condition that it shall not, by way of trade or otherwise, be lent,
re-sold, hired out, or otherwise circulated without the publisher's
prior consent in any form of binding or cover other than that in
which it is published and without a similar condition including this
condition being imposed on the subsequent purchaser

978-0-141-19109-6

www.greenpenguin.co.uk

MIX
Paper | Supporting
responsible forestry
FSC® C018179

Penguin Books is committed to a sustainable
future for our business, our readers and our planet.
This book is made from Forest Stewardship
Council™ certified paper.

Contents

Suddenly Last Summer 1

The Milk Train Doesn't Stop Here Anymore 53

Small Craft Warnings 153

Suddenly Last Summer

Scene One

The set may be as unrealistic as the decor of a dramatic ballet. It represents part of a mansion of Victorian Gothic style in the Garden District of New Orleans on a late afternoon, between late summer and early fall. The interior is blended with a fantastic garden which is more like a tropical jungle, or forest, in the prehistoric age of giant fern-forests when living creatures had flippers turning to limbs and scales to skin. The colours of this jungle-garden are violent, especially since it is steaming with heat after rain. There are massive tree-flowers that suggest organs of a body, torn out, still glistening with undried blood; there are harsh cries and sibilant hissings and thrashing sounds in the garden as if it were inhabited by beasts, serpents, and birds, all of savage nature . . .

> [*The jungle tumult continues a few moments after the curtain rises; then subsides into relative quiet, which is occasionally broken by a new outburst.*
>
> *A lady enters with the assistance of a silver-knobbed cane. She has light orange or pink hair and wears a lavender lace dress, and over her withered bosom is pinned a starfish of diamonds.*
>
> *She is followed by a young blond* DOCTOR, *all in white, glacially brilliant, very, very good-looking, and the old lady's manner and eloquence indicate her undeliberate response to his icy charm.*]

MRS VENABLE: Yes, this was Sebastian's garden. The Latin names of the plants were printed on tags attached to them but the print's fading out. Those ones there – [*She draws a deep breath.*] – are the oldest plants on earth, survivors from the age of the giant fern-forests. Of course in this semi-tropical climate – [*She takes another deep breath.*] – some of the rarest plants, such as the

3

Venus flytrap – you know what this is, Doctor? The Venus fly-trap?

DOCTOR: An insectivorous plant?

MRS VENABLE: Yes, it feeds on insects. It has to be kept under glass from early fall to late spring and when it went under glass, my son, Sebastian, had to provide it with fruit flies flown in at great expense from a Florida laboratory that used fruit flies for experiments in genetics. Well, I can't do that, Doctor. [*She takes a deep breath.*] I can't, I just can't do it! It's not the expense but the –

DOCTOR: Effort.

MRS VENABLE: Yes. So goodbye, Venus flytrap! – like so much else . . . Whew! . . . [*She draws breath.*] – I don't know why, but –! I already feel I can lean on your shoulder, Doctor – Cu? – Cu?

DOCTOR: Cu-kro-wicz. It's a Polish word that means sugar, so let's make it simple and call me Doctor Sugar. [*He returns her smile.*]

MRS VENABLE: Well, now, Doctor Sugar, you've seen Sebastian's garden.

[*They are advancing slowly to the patio area.*]

DOCTOR: It's like a well-groomed jungle . . .

MRS VENABLE: That's how he meant it to be, nothing was accidental, everything was planned and designed in Sebastian's life and his – [*She dabs her forehead with her handkerchief, which she had taken from her reticule.*] – work!

DOCTOR: What was your son's work, Mrs Venable? – besides this garden?

MRS VENABLE: As many times as I've had to answer that question! D'you know it still shocks me a little? – to realize that Sebastian Venable the poet is still unknown outside of a small coterie of friends, including his mother.

DOCTOR: Oh.

MRS VENABLE: You see, strictly speaking, his *life* was his occupation.

DOCTOR: I see.

MRS VENABLE: No, you *don't* see, yet, but before I'm through, you will. – Sebastian was a poet? That's what I meant when I said his life was his work because the work of a poet is the life of a poet, and – vice versa, the life of a poet is the work of a poet, I mean you can't separate them, I mean – well, for instance, a salesman's work is one thing and his life is another – or can be. The same thing's true of – doctor, lawyer, merchant, *thief*! – But a poet's life is his work and his work is his life in a special sense because – oh, I've already talked myself breathless and dizzy.

[*The* DOCTOR *offers his arm.*]

Thank you.

DOCTOR: Mrs Venable, did your doctor okay this thing?

MRS VENABLE [*breathless*]: What thing?

DOCTOR: Your meeting this girl that you think is responsible for your son's death?

MRS VENABLE: I've waited months to face her because I couldn't get to St Mary's to face her – I've had her brought here to my house. I won't collapse! She'll collapse! I mean her lies will collapse – not my truth – not the truth . . . *Forward march, Doctor Sugar!*

[*He conducts her slowly to the patio.*]

Ah, we've *made* it, *ha ha*! I didn't know that I was so weak on my pins! Sit down, Doctor. I'm not afraid of using every last ounce and inch of my little, left-over strength in doing just what I'm doing. I'm devoting all that's left of my life, Doctor, to the defence of a dead poet's reputation. Sebastian had no public name as a poet, he didn't want one, he refused to have one. He *dreaded, abhorred*! – false values that come from being publicly known, from fame, from personal – exploitation . . . Oh, he'd say to me: 'Violet? Mother? – You're going to outlive me!!'

DOCTOR: What made him think that?

MRS VENABLE: Poets are always clairvoyant! – And he had rheumatic fever when he was fifteen and it affected a heart-valve and he wouldn't stay off horses and out of water and so forth . . . 'Violet? Mother? You're going to live longer than me, and then, when I'm gone, it will be yours, in your hands, to do whatever you please with!' – Meaning, of course, his future recognition! – That he *did* want, he wanted it after his death when it couldn't disturb him;

then he did want to offer his work to the world. All right. Have I made my point, Doctor? Well, here is my son's work, Doctor, here's his life going *on*!

[*She lifts a thin gilt-edged volume from the patio table as if elevating the Host before the altar. Its gold leaf and lettering catch the afternoon sun. It says* Poem of Summer. *Her face suddenly has a different look, the look of a visionary, an exalted* religieuse. *At the same instant a bird sings clearly and purely in the garden and the old lady seems to be almost young for a moment.*]

DOCTOR [*reading the title*]: *Poem of Summer?*

MRS VENABLE: *Poem of Summer*, and the date of the summer, there are twenty-five of them, he wrote one poem a year which he printed himself on an eighteenth-century handpress at his – *atelier* in the – French – Quarter – so no one but he could see it . . .

[*She seems dizzy for a moment.*]

DOCTOR: He wrote one poem a year?

MRS VENABLE: One for each summer that we travelled together. The other nine months of the year were really only a preparation.

DOCTOR: Nine months?

MRS VENABLE: The length of a pregnancy, yes . . .

DOCTOR: The poem was hard to deliver?

MRS VENABLE: Yes, even with me! *Without* me, *impossible*, Doctor! – he wrote no poem last summer.

DOCTOR: He died last summer?

MRS VENABLE: Without me he died last summer, that was his last summer's poem. [*She staggers; he assists her toward a chair. She catches her breath with difficulty.*] One long-ago summer – now, why am I thinking of this? – my son, Sebastian, said, 'Mother? – Listen to this!' – He read me Herman Melville's description of the Encantadas, the Galapagos Islands. Quote – take five and twenty heaps of cinders dumped here and there in an outside city lot. Imagine some of them magnified into mountains, and the vacant lot, the sea. And you'll have a fit idea of the general aspect of the Encantadas, the Enchanted Isles – extinct volcanoes, looking much as the world at large might look – after a last conflagration – end quote. He read me that description and said that we had to go there. And so we did go there that summer on a chartered boat, a four-masted schooner, as close as possible to the sort of a boat that Melville must have sailed on . . . We saw the Encantadas, but on the Encantadas we saw something Melville *hadn't* written about. We saw the great sea-turtles crawl up out of the sea for their annual egg-laying . . . Once a year the female of the sea-turtle crawls up out of the equatorial sea on to the blazing sand-beach of a volcanic island to dig a pit in the sand and deposit her eggs there. It's a long and dreadful thing, the depositing of the eggs in the sand-pits, and when it's finished the exhausted female turtle crawls back to the sea half-dead. She never sees her offspring, but we did. Sebastian knew exactly when the sea-turtle eggs would be hatched out and we returned in time for it . . .

DOCTOR: You went back to the –?

MRS VENABLE: Terrible Encantadas, those heaps of extinct volcanoes, in time to witness the hatching of the sea-turtles and their desperate flight to the sea!

[*There is a sound of harsh bird-cries in the air. She looks up.*]

– The narrow beach, the colour of caviar, was all in motion! But the sky was in motion, too . . .

DOCTOR: The sky was in motion, too?

MRS VENABLE: – Full of flesh-eating birds and the noise of the birds, the horrible savage cries of the –

DOCTOR: Carnivorous birds?

MRS VENABLE: Over the narrow black heath of the Encantadas as the just-hatched sea-turtles scrambled out of the sand-pits and started their race to the sea . . .

DOCTOR: Race to the sea?

MRS VENABLE: To escape the flesh-eating birds that made the sky almost as black as the beach!

[*She gazes up again; we hear the wild, ravenous, harsh cries of the birds. The sound comes in rhythmic waves like a savage chant.*]

7

And the sand all alive, all alive, as the hatched sea-turtles made their dash for the sea, while the birds hovered and swooped to attack and hovered and – swooped to attack! They were diving down on the hatched sea-turtles, turning sides open and rending and eating their flesh. Sebastian guessed that possibly only a hundredth of one per cent of their number would escape to the sea . . .

DOCTOR: What was it about this that fascinated your son?

MRS VENABLE: My son was looking for – [*She stops short with a slight gasp.*] – Let's just say he was interested in sea-turtles!

DOCTOR: That isn't what you started to say.

MRS VENABLE: I stopped myself just in time.

DOCTOR: Say what you started to say.

MRS VENABLE: I started to say that my son was looking for God and I stopped myself because I thought you'd think 'Oh, a pretentious young crackpot!' – which Sebastian was *not*!

DOCTOR: Mrs Venable, doctors look for God, too.

MRS VENABLE: Oh?

DOCTOR: I think they have to look harder for him than priests since they don't have the help of such well-known guide-books and well-organized expeditions as the priests have with their scriptures and – churches . . .

MRS VENABLE: You mean they go on a solitary safari like a poet?

DOCTOR: Yes. Some do. I do.

MRS VENABLE: I believe, I *believe* you! [*She laughs, startled.*]

DOCTOR: Let me tell you something – the first operation I performed at Lion's View. – You can imagine how anxious and nervous I was about the outcome.

MRS VENABLE: Yes.

DOCTOR: The patient was a young girl regarded as hopeless and put in the Drum –

MRS VENABLE: Yes.

DOCTOR: The name for the violent ward at Lion's View because it looks like the inside of a drum with very bright lights burning all day and all night. – So the attendants can see any change of expression or movement among the inmates in time to grab them if they're about to attack. After the operation I stayed with the girl, as if I'd delivered a child that might stop breathing. – When they finally wheeled her out of the surgery, I still stayed with her. I walked along by the rolling table holding on to her hand – with my heart in my throat.

[*We hear faint music.*]

– It was a nice afternoon, as fair as this one. And the moment we wheeled her outside, she whispered something, she whispered: 'Oh, how blue the sky is!' – And I felt proud, I felt proud and relieved because up till then her speech, everything that she'd babbled, was a torrent of obscenities!

MRS VENABLE: Yes, well, now, I can tell you without any hesitation that my son *was* looking for God, I mean for a clear image of Him. He spent that whole blazing equatorial day in the crow's-nest of the schooner watching this thing on the beach till it was too dark to see it, and when he came down the rigging he said 'Well, now I've seen Him!', and he meant God. – And for several weeks after that he had a fever, he was delirious with it –

[*The Encantadas music then fades in again, briefly, at a lower level, a whisper.*]

DOCTOR: I can see how he *might* be, I think he *would* be disturbed if he thought he'd seen God's image, an equation of God, in that spectacle you watched in the Encantadas: creatures of the air hovering over and swooping down to devour creatures of the sea that had had the bad luck to be hatched on land and weren't able to scramble back into the sea fast enough to escape that massacre you witnessed, yes, I can see how such a spectacle could be equated with a good deal of – *experience, existence*! – but not with *God*! Can *you*?

MRS VENABLE: Dr Sugar, I'm a reasonably loyal member of the Protestant Episcopal Church, but I understood what he meant.

DOCTOR: Did he mean we must rise above God?

MRS VENABLE: He meant that God shows a savage face to people and shouts some fierce things at them, it's all we see or hear of Him. Isn't it all we ever really see and hear of Him, now? – Nobody seems to know why . . .

[*Music fades out again.*]

Shall I go on from there?

DOCTOR: Yes, do.

MRS VENABLE: Well, next? – India – China –

[MISS FOXHILL *appears with the medicine.* MRS VENABLE *sees her.*]

FOXHILL: Mrs Venable.

MRS VENABLE: Oh, God – elixir of – [*She takes the glass.*] Isn't it kind of the drugstore to keep me alive. Where was I, Doctor?

DOCTOR: In the Himalayas.

MRS VENABLE: Oh yes, that long-ago summer . . . In the Himalayas he almost entered a Buddhist monastery, had gone so far as to shave his head and eat just rice out of a wood bowl on a grass mat. He'd promised those sly Buddhist monks that he would give up the world and himself and all his worldly possessions to their mendicant order. – Well, I cabled his father, 'For God's sake notify bank to freeze Sebastian's accounts!' – I got back this cable from my late husband's lawyer: 'Mr Venable critically ill Stop Wants you Stop Needs you Stop Immediate return advised most strongly Stop Cable time of arrival . . .'

DOCTOR: Did you go back to your husband?

MRS VENABLE: I made the hardest decision of my life. I stayed with my son. I got him through that crisis too. In less than a month he got up off the filthy grass mat and threw the rice bowl away – and booked us into Shepheard's Hotel in Cairo and the Ritz in Paris – And from then on, oh, we – still lived in a – world of light and shadow . . . [*She turns vaguely with empty glass. He rises and takes it from her.*] But the shadow was almost as luminous as the light.

DOCTOR: Don't you want to sit down now?

MRS VENABLE: Yes, indeed I do, before I fall down.

[*He assists her into wheelchair.*]

– Are your hind-legs still on you?

DOCTOR [*still concerned over her agitation*]: – My what? Oh – hind-legs! – Yes . . .

MRS VENABLE: Well, then you're not a donkey, you're certainly not a donkey because I've been talking the hind-legs off a donkey – several donkeys . . . But I had to make it clear to you that the world lost a great deal too when I lost my son last summer . . . You would have liked my son; he would have been charmed by you. My son, Sebastian, was not a family snob or a money snob, but he was a snob, all right. He was a snob about personal charm in people, he insisted upon good looks in people around him, and, oh, he had a perfect little court of young and beautiful people around him always, wherever he was, here in New *Orleans* or New York or on the Riviera or in Paris and Venice, he always had a little entourage of the beautiful and the talented and the young!

DOCTOR: Your son was young, Mrs Venable?

MRS VENABLE: Both of us were young, and stayed young, Doctor.

DOCTOR: Could I see a photograph of your son, Mrs Venable?

MRS VENABLE: Yes, indeed you could, Doctor. I'm glad that you asked to see one. I'm going to show you not one photograph but two. Here. Here is my son, Sebastian, in a Renaissance page-boy's costume at a masked ball in Cannes. Here is my son, Sebastian, in the same costume at a masked ball in Venice. These two pictures were taken twenty years apart. Now which is the older one, Doctor?

DOCTOR: This photograph looks older.

MRS VENABLE: The photograph looks older, but not the subject. It takes character to refuse to grow old, Doctor – successfully to refuse to. It calls for discipline, abstention. One cocktail before dinner, not two, four, six – a single lean chop and lime juice on a salad in restaurants famed for rich dishes.

[FOXHILL *comes from the house.*]

FOXHILL: Mrs Venable, Miss Holly's mother and brother are –

[*Simultaneously* MRS HOLLY *and* GEORGE *appear in the window.*]

GEORGE: Hi, Aunt Vi!

MRS HOLLY: Violet dear, we're here.

FOXHILL: They're here.

MRS VENABLE: Wait upstairs in my upstairs living-room for me. [*To*

MISS FOXHILL] Get them upstairs. I don't want them at that window during this talk. [*To the* DOCTOR] Let's get away from the window.

[*He wheels her to stage centre.*]

DOCTOR: Mrs Venable? Did your son have a – well – what kind of a *personal*, well, *private* life did –

MRS VENABLE: That's a question I wanted you to ask me.

DOCTOR: Why?

MRS VENABLE: I haven't heard the girl's story except indirectly in a watered-down version, being too ill to go to hear it directly, but I've gathered enough to know that it's a hideous attack on my son's moral character which, being dead, he can't defend himself from. I have to be the defender. Now. Sit down. Listen to me . . .

[*The* DOCTOR *sits.*]

. . . before you hear whatever you're going to hear from the girl when she gets here. My son, Sebastian, was chaste. Not c-h-a-s-e-d! Oh, he was chased in that way of spelling it, too, we had to be very fleet-footed I can tell you, with his looks and his charm, to keep ahead of pursuers, every kind of pursuer! – I mean he was c-h-a-s-t-e! – Chaste . . .

DOCTOR: I understood what you meant, Mrs Venable.

MRS VENABLE: And you *believe* me, don't you?

DOCTOR: Yes, but –

MRS VENABLE: But *what*?

DOCTOR: Chastity at – what age was your son last summer?

MRS VENABLE: *Forty*, maybe. We really didn't count birthdays . . .

DOCTOR: He lived a celibate life?

MRS VENABLE: As strictly as if he'd *vowed* to! This sounds like vanity, Doctor, but really I was actually the only one in his life that satisfied the demands he made of people. Time after time my son would let people go, dismiss them! – because their, their, their! – *attitude* toward him was –

DOCTOR: Not as pure as –

MRS VENABLE: My son, Sebastian, demanded! We were a famous couple. People didn't speak of Sebastian and his mother or Mrs

Venable and her son, they said, 'Sebastian and Violet, Violet and Sebastian are staying at the Lido, they're at the Ritz in Madrid. Sebastian and Violet, Violet and Sebastian have taken a house at Biarritz for the season,' and every appearance, every time we appeared, attention was centred on *us*! – *everyone else! Eclipsed!* Vanity? Ohhhh, no, Doctor, you can't call it that –

DOCTOR: I didn't call it that.

MRS VENABLE: – It wasn't *folie de grandeur*, it was grandeur.

DOCTOR: I see.

MRS VENABLE: An attitude toward life that's hardly been known in the world since the great Renaissance princes were crowded out of their palaces and gardens by successful shopkeepers!

DOCTOR: I see.

MRS VENABLE: Most people's lives – what are they but trails of debris, each day more debris, more debris, long, long trails of debris with nothing to clean it all up but, finally, death . . .

[*We hear lyric music.*]

My son, Sebastian, and I constructed our days, each day, we would – carve out each day of our lives like a piece of sculpture. – Yes, we left behind us a trail of days like a gallery of sculpture! But, last summer –

[*Pause: the music continues.*]

I can't forgive him for it, not even now that he's paid for it with his life! – he let in this – *vandal*! This –

DOCTOR: The girl that –?

MRS VENABLE: That you're going to meet here this afternoon! Yes. He admitted this vandal and with her tongue for a hatchet she's gone about smashing our legend, the memory of –

DOCTOR: Mrs Venable, what do you think is her reason?

MRS VENABLE: Lunatics don't have reason!

DOCTOR: I mean, what do you think is her – motive?

MRS VENABLE: What a question! – We put the bread in her mouth and the clothes on her back. People that like you for that or even forgive you for it are, are – *hen's teeth*, Doctor. The role of the benefactor is worse than thankless, it's the role of a victim, Doctor, a sacrificial victim, yes, they want your blood, Doctor, they want your blood on the altar steps of their *outraged, outrageous* egos!

DOCTOR: Oh. You mean she resented the –

MRS VENABLE: Loathed! – They can't shut her up at St Mary's.

DOCTOR: I thought she'd been there for months.

MRS VENABLE: I mean keep her *still* there. She *babbles*! They couldn't shut her up in Cabeza de Lobo or at the clinic in Paris – she babbled, babbled! – smashing my son's reputation. – On the *Berengaria* bringing her back to the States she broke out of the state room and babbled, babbled; even at the airport when she was flown down here, she babbled a bit of her story before they could whisk her into an ambulance to St Mary's. This is a reticule, Doctor. [*She raises a cloth bag.*] A catch-all, carry-all bag for an elderly lady which I turned into last summer . . . . Will you open it for me, my hands are stiff, and fish out some cigarettes and a cigarette holder.

[*He does.*]

DOCTOR: I don't have matches.

MRS VENABLE: I think there's a table-lighter on the table.

DOCTOR: Yes, there is. [*He lights it, it flames up high.*] My Lord, what a torch!

MRS VENABLE [*with a sudden, sweet smile*]: 'So shines a good deed in a naughty world,' Doctor – Sugar . . .

[*Pause. A bird sings sweetly in the garden.*]

DOCTOR: Mrs Venable?

MRS VENABLE: Yes?

DOCTOR: In your letter last week you made some reference to a, to a – fund of some kind, an endowment fund of –

MRS VENABLE: I wrote you that my lawyers and bankers and certified public accountants were setting up the Sebastian Venable Memorial Foundation to subsidize the work of young people like you that are pushing out the frontiers of art and science, but have a financial problem. You have a financial problem, don't you, Doctor?

DOCTOR: Yes, we do have that problem. My work is such a *new* and *radical* thing that people in charge of state funds are naturally a little scared of it and keep us on a small budget, so small that – We need a separate ward for my patients, I need trained assistants, I'd like to marry a girl I can't afford to marry! – But there's also the problem of getting right patients, not just – criminal psychopaths that the State turns over to us for my operation! – because it's – well – risky . . . I don't want to turn you against my work at Lion's View, but I have to be honest with you. There is a good deal of risk in my operation. Whenever you enter the brain with a foreign object . . .

MRS VENABLE: Yes.

DOCTOR: – Even a needle-thin knife . . .

MRS VENABLE: Yes.

DOCTOR: In a skilled surgeon's fingers . . .

MRS VENABLE: Yes.

DOCTOR: – There is a good deal of risk involved in – the operation . . .

MRS VENABLE: You said that it pacifies them, it quiets them down, it suddenly makes them peaceful.

DOCTOR: Yes. It does that, that much we already know, but –

MRS VENABLE: What?

DOCTOR: Well, it will be ten years before we can tell if the immediate benefits of the operation will be lasting or – passing or even if there'd still be – and this is what haunts me about it! – any possibility, afterwards, of – reconstructing a – totally sound person, it may be that the person will always be limited afterwards, relieved of acute disturbances but – *limited*, Mrs Venable . . .

MRS VENABLE: Oh, but what a blessing to them, Doctor, to be just peaceful, to be just suddenly – peaceful . . .

[*A bird sings sweetly in the garden.*]

After all that horror, after those nightmares: just to be able to lift up their eyes and see – [*She looks up and raises a hand to indicate the sky.*] – a sky not as black with savage, devouring birds as the sky that we saw in the Encantadas, Doctor.

DOCTOR: – Mrs Venable? I can't guarantee that a lobotomy would stop her – *babbling*!!

MRS VENABLE: That may be, maybe not, but after the operation, who would *believe* her, Doctor?

[*Pause; faint jungle music.*]

DOCTOR [*quietly*]: My God.

[*Pause.*]

Mrs Venable, suppose after meeting the girl and observing the girl and hearing this story she babbles – I still shouldn't feel that her condition's – intractable enough! to justify the risks of – suppose I shouldn't feel that non-surgical treatment such as insulin shock and electric shock and –

MRS VENABLE: SHE'S HAD ALL THAT AT ST MARY'S!! Nothing else is left for her.

DOCTOR: But if I disagreed with you?

[*Pause.*]

MRS VENABLE: That's just part of a question: finish the question, Doctor.

DOCTOR: Would you still be interested in my work at Lion's View? I mean would the Sebastian Venable Memorial Foundation still be interested in it?

MRS VENABLE: Aren't we always more interested in a thing that concerns us personally, Doctor?

DOCTOR: Mrs Venable!!

[CATHARINE HOLLY *appears between the lace window curtains.*]

You're such an innocent person that it doesn't occur to you, it obviously hasn't even occurred to you that anybody less innocent than you are could possibly interpret this offer of a subsidy as – well, as sort of a *bribe*?

MRS VENABLE [*laughs, throwing her bead back*]: Name it that – I don't care – There's just two things to remember. She's a destroyer. My son was a *creator*! – Now if my honesty's shocked you – pick up your little black bag without the subsidy in it, and run away from this garden! – Nobody's heard our conversation but you and I,

Doctor Sugar . . .

[MISS FOXHILL *comes out of the house and calls.*]

MISS FOXHILL: Mrs Venable?
MRS VENABLE: What is it, what do you want, Miss Foxhill?
MISS FOXHILL: Mrs Venable? Miss Holly is here, with –

[MRS VENABLE *sees* CATHARINE *at the window.*]

MRS VENABLE: Oh, my God. There she is, in the window! – I told you I didn't want her to enter my house again. I told you to meet them at the door and lead them around the side of the house to the garden, and you didn't listen. I'm not ready to face her. I have to have my five o'clock cocktail first, to fortify me. Take my chair inside. Doctor? Are you still here? I thought you'd run out of the garden. I'm going back through the garden to the other entrance. Doctor Sugar? You may stay in the garden if you wish to or run out of the garden if you wish to or go in this way if you wish to or do anything that you wish to but I'm going to have my five o'clock daiquiri, *frozen!* – before I face her . . .

[*All during this she has been sailing very slowly off through the garden like a stately vessel at sea with a fair wind in her sails, a pirate's frigate or a treasure-laden galleon. The young* DOCTOR *stares at* CATHARINE *framed by the lace window curtains.* SISTER FELICITY *appears beside her and draws her away from the window. Music: an ominous fanfare.* SISTER FELICITY *holds the door open for* CATHARINE *as the* DOCTOR *starts quickly forward. He starts to pick up his bag, but doesn't.* CATHARINE *rushes out, they almost collide with each other.*]

CATHARINE: Excuse me.
DOCTOR: I'm sorry . . .

[*She looks after him as he goes into the house.*]

SISTER FELICITY: Sit down and be still till your family come outside.

DIM OUT

Scene Two

[CATHARINE *removes a cigarette from a lacquered box on the table and lights it. The following quick, cadenced lines are accompanied by quick, dancelike movement, almost formal, as the* SISTER *in her sweeping white habit, which should be starched to make a crackling sound, pursues the girl about the white wicker patio table and among the wicker chairs: this can be accompanied by quick music.*]

SISTER: What did you take out of that box on the table?

CATHARINE: Just a cigarette, Sister.

SISTER: Put it back in the box.

CATHARINE: Too late, it's already lighted.

SISTER: Give it here.

CATHARINE: Oh, please, let me smoke, Sister!

SISTER: Give it here.

CATHARINE: *Please*, Sister Felicity.

SISTER: Catharine, give it here. You know that you're not allowed to smoke at St Mary's.

CATHARINE: We're not at St Mary's, this is an afternoon out.

SISTER: You're still in my charge. I can't permit you to smoke because the last time you smoked you dropped a lighted cigarette on your dress and started a fire.

CATHARINE: Oh, I did not start a fire. I just burned a hole in my skirt because I was half unconscious under medication.

[*She is now behind a white wicker chair.*]

SISTER [*overlapping her*]: Catharine, give it here.

CATHARINE: Don't be such a bully!

SISTER: Disobedience has to be paid for later.

CATHARINE: All right, I'll pay for it later.

SISTER [*overlapping*]: Give me that cigarette or I'll make a report that'll put you right back on the violent ward, if you don't. [*She claps her hands twice and holds one hand out across the table.*]

CATHARINE [*overlapping*]: I'm not being violent, Sister.

SISTER [*overlapping*]: Give me that cigarette, I'm holding my hand out for it!

CATHARINE: All right, take it, here, take it!

[*She thrusts the lighted end of the cigarette into the palm of the* SISTER's *hand. The* SISTER *cries out and sucks her burned hand.*]

SISTER: *You burned me with it!*

CATHARINE: I'm sorry, I didn't mean to.

SISTER [*shocked, hurt*]: You deliberately burned me!

CATHARINE [*overlapping*]: You said give it to you and so I gave it to you.

SISTER [*overlapping*]: You stuck the lighted end of that cigarette in my hand!

CATHARINE [*overlapping*]: I'm *sick*, I'm *sick*! – of being *bossed* and *bullied*!

SISTER [*commandingly*]: *Sit down!*

[CATHARINE *sits down stiffly in a white wicker chair on forestage, facing the audience. The* SISTER *resumes sucking the burned palm of her hand. Ten beats. Then from inside the house the whirr of a mechanical mixer.*]

CATHARINE: There goes the Waring Mixer, Aunt Violet's about to have her five o'clock frozen daiquiri, you could set a watch by it! [*She almost laughs. Then she draws a deep, shuddering breath and leans back in her chair, but her hands remain clenched on the white wicker arms.*]

– We're in Sebastian's garden. *My God, I can still cry!*

SISTER: Did you have any medication before you went out?

CATHARINE: No. I didn't have any. Will you give me some, Sister?

SISTER [*almost gently*]: I can't. I wasn't told to. However, I think the doctor will give you something.

CATHARINE: The young blond man I bumped into?

SISTER: Yes. The young doctor's a specialist from another hospital.

CATHARINE: What hospital?

SISTER: A word to the wise is sufficient . . .

[*The* DOCTOR *has appeared in the window.*]

CATHARINE [*rising abruptly*]: I knew I was being watched, he's in the window, staring out at me!

SISTER: Sit down and be still. Your family's coming outside.

CATHARINE [*overlapping*]: LION'S VIEW, IS IT! DOCTOR?

[*She has advanced toward the bay window. The* DOCTOR *draws back, letting the misty white gauze curtains down to obscure him.*]

SISTER [*rising with a restraining gesture which is almost pitying*]: Sit down, dear.

CATHARINE: IS IT LION'S VIEW? DOCTOR?

SISTER: Be still . . .

CATHARINE: WHEN CAN I STOP RUNNING DOWN THAT STEEP WHITE STREET IN CABEZA DE LOBO?

SISTER: Catharine, dear, sit down.

CATHARINE: I loved him, Sister! Why wouldn't he let me save him? I tried to hold on to his hand, but he struck me away and ran, ran, ran in the wrong direction, Sister!

SISTER: Catharine, dear – be still.

[*The* SISTER *sneezes.*]

CATHARINE: Bless you, Sister. [*She says this absently, still watching the window.*]

SISTER: Thank you.

CATHARINE: The Doctor's still at the window but he's too blond to hide behind window curtains, he catches the light, he shines through them. [*She turns from the window.*] – We were *going* to blonds, blonds were next on the menu.

SISTER: Be still now. Quiet, dear.

CATHARINE: Cousin Sebastian said he was famished for blonds, he was fed-up with the dark ones and was famished for blonds. All the travel brochures he picked up were advertisements of the blond northern countries. I think he'd already booked us to – Copenhagen or – Stockholm. – Fed up with dark ones, famished for light ones: that's how he talked about people, as if they were – items on a menu, – 'That one's delicious-looking, that one is appetizing,' or 'that one is *not* appetizing' – I think because he was really nearly half-starved from living on pills and salads . . .

SISTER: *Stop it!* – Catharine, be still.

CATHARINE: He liked me and so I loved him . . . [*She cries a little again.*] If he'd kept hold of my hand I could have saved him! – Sebastian suddenly said to me last summer: 'Let's fly north, little bird – I want to walk under those radiant, cold northern lights – I've never *seen* the aurora borealis!' – Somebody said once or wrote, once: 'We're all of us children in a vast kindergarten trying to spell God's name with the wrong alphabet blocks!'

MRS HOLLY [*offstage*]: *Sister?*

   [*The* SISTER *rises.*]

CATHARINE [*rising*]: I think it's *me* they're calling, they call *me* 'Sister', Sister!

Scene Three

[*The* SISTER *resumes her seat impassively as the girl's mother and younger brother appear from the garden. The mother,* MRS HOLLY, *is a fatuous Southern lady who requires no other description. The brother,* GEORGE, *is typically good-looking, he has the best 'looks' of the family, tall and elegant of figure. They enter.*]

MRS HOLLY: Catharine, dear! Catharine – [*They embrace tentatively.*] Well, well! Doesn't she look fine, George?

GEORGE: Uh huh.

CATHARINE: They send you to the beauty parlour whenever you're going to have a family visit. Other times you look awful, you can't have a compact or lipstick or anything made out of metal because they're afraid you'll swallow it.

MRS HOLLY [*giving a tinkly little laugh*]: I think she looks just splendid, don't you, George?

GEORGE: Can't we talk to her without the nun for a minute?

MRS HOLLY: Yes, I'm sure it's all right to. Sister?

CATHARINE: Excuse me, Sister Felicity, this is my mother, Mrs Holly, and my brother, George.

SISTER: How do you do.

GEORGE: How d'ya do.

CATHARINE: This is Sister Felicity . . .

MRS HOLLY: We're so happy that Catharine's at St Mary's! So very grateful for all you're doing for her.

SISTER [*sadly, mechanically*]: We do the best we can for her, Mrs Holly.

MRS HOLLY: I'm sure you do. Yes, well – I wonder if you would mind if we had a little private chat with our Cathie?

SISTER: I'm not supposed to let her out of my sight.

MRS HOLLY: It's just for a minute. You can sit in the hall or the garden and we'll call you right back here the minute the private part of the little talk is over.

[SISTER FELICITY *withdraws with an uncertain nod and a swish of starched fabric.*]

GEORGE [*to Catharine*]: *Jesus! What are you up to? Huh! Sister? Are you trying to* RUIN *us?!*

MRS HOLLY: GAWGE! WILL YOU BE QUIET. You're upsetting your sister!

[*He jumps up and stalks off a little, rapping his knee with his zipper-covered tennis racket.*]

CATHARINE: How elegant George looks!

MRS HOLLY: George inherited Cousin Sebastian's wardrobe, but everything else is in probate! Did you know that? That everything else is in probate, and Violet can keep it in probate just as long as she wants to?

CATHARINE: Where is Aunt Violet?

MRS HOLLY: *George, come back here!*

[*He does, sulkily.*]

Violet's on her way down.

GEORGE: Yeah, Aunt Violet has an elevator now.

MRS HOLLY: Yais, she has, she's had an elevator installed where the back stairs were, and, Sister, it's the cutest little thing you ever did see! It's panelled in Chinese lacquer, black an' gold Chinese lacquer, with lovely bird-pictures on it. But there's only room for two people at a time in it. George and I came down on foot. – I think she's havin' her frozen daiquiri now, she still has a frozen daiquiri promptly at five o'clock ev'ry afternoon in the world . . . in warm weather . . . Sister, the horrible death of Sebastian just about *killed* her! – She's now slightly better . . . but it's a question of time. – Dear, you know, I'm sure that you understand, why we haven't been out to see you at St Mary's. They said you were too disturbed, and a family visit might disturb you more. But I want you to know that nobody, absolutely nobody in the city, knows a thing about what you've been through. Have they, George? Not a thing. Not a soul even knows that you've come back from Europe. When people inquire, when they question us about you, we just say that you've stayed abroad to study something or other. [*She catches her breath.*] Now. Sister? – I want you to please be *very* careful what you say to your Aunt Violet about what happened to Sebastian in Cabeza de Lobo.

CATHARINE: What do you want me to say about what – ?

MRS HOLLY: Just don't repeat that same fantastic story! For my sake and George's sake, the sake of your brother and mother, don't repeat that horrible story again! Not to Violet! Will you?

CATHARINE: Then I am going to have to tell Aunt Violet what happened to her son in Cabeza de Lobo?

MRS HOLLY: Honey, that's why you're here. She has INSISTED on hearing it straight from YOU!

GEORGE: You were the only witness to it, Cathie.

CATHARINE: No, there were others. That *ran.*

MRS HOLLY: Oh, Sister, you've just had a little sort of a – *nightmare* about it! Now, listen to me, will you, Sister? Sebastian has left, has BEQUEATHED! – to you an' Gawge in his *will* –

GEORGE [*religiously*]: *To each of us, fifty grand, each!* – AFTER TAXES! – GET IT?

CATHARINE: Oh, yes, but if they give me an injection – I won't have any choice but to tell exactly what happened in Cabeza de Lobo last summer. Don't you see? I won't have any choice but to tell the truth. It makes you tell the truth because it shuts something off that might make you able not to and *everything* comes out, decent or *not* decent, you have no control, but always, always the truth!

MRS HOLLY: Catharine, darling. I don't know the full story, but surely you're not too sick in your *head* to know in your *heart* that the story you've been telling is just – too –

GEORGE [*cutting in*]: Cathie, Cathie, you got to forget that story! Can'tcha? For *your* fifty grand?

MRS HOLLY: Because if Aunt Vi contests the will, and we know she'll contest it, she'll keep it in the courts for ever! – We'll be –

GEORGE: It's in PROBATE NOW! And'll never get out of probate until you drop that story – we can't afford to hire lawyers good enough to contest it! So if you don't stop telling that crazy story, we won't have a pot to – cook *greens* in!

[*He turns away with a fierce grimace and a sharp, abrupt wave of his hand, as if slapping down something.* CATHERINE *stares at his tall back for a moment and laughs wildly.*]

MRS HOLLY: Catharine, don't laugh like that; it scares me, Catharine.

[*Jungle birds scream in the garden.*]

GEORGE [*turning his back on his sister*]: Cathie, the money is all tied up.

[*He stoops over sofa, hands on flannel knees, speaking directly into* CATHARINE's *face as if she were hard of hearing. She raises a hand to touch his cheek affectionately; he seizes the hand and removes it but holds it tight.*]

If Aunt Vi decided to contest Sebastian's will that leaves us all of this cash?! – Am I coming through to you?

CATHARINE: Yes, little brother, you are.

GEORGE: You see, Mama, she's crazy like a coyote! [*He gives her a quick cold kiss.*] We won't get a single damn penny, honest t' God we won't! So you've just GOT to stop tellin' that story about what you say happened to Cousin Sebastian in Cabeza de Lobo, even if it's what it *couldn't* be, TRUE! – You got to drop it, Sister, you can't tell such a story to civilized people in a civilized up-to-date country!

MRS HOLLY: Cathie, why, why, why! – did you invent such a tale?

CATHARINE: But, Mother, I DIDN'T invent it. I know it's a hideous story but it's a true story of our time and the world we live in and what did truly happen to Cousin Sebastian in Cabeza de Lobo . . .

GEORGE: Oh, then you are going to tell it. Mama, she IS going to tell it! Right to Aunt Vi, and lose us a hundred thousand! – Cathie? You are a BITCH!

MRS HOLLY: GAWGE!

GEORGE: I repeat it, a bitch! She isn't crazy, Mama, she's no more crazy than I am, she's just, just – PERVERSE! Was ALWAYS – perverse . . .

[CATHARINE *turns away and breaks into quiet sobbing.*]

MRS HOLLY: Gawge, Gawge, apologize to Sister, this is no way for you to talk to your sister. You come right back over here and tell your sweet little sister you're sorry you spoke like that to her!

GEORGE [*turning back to* CATHARINE]: I'm sorry, Cathie, but you know we NEED that money! Mama and me, we – Cathie? I got *ambitions*! And, Cathie, I'm YOUNG! – I *want* things, I *need* them, Cathie! So will you please think about Me? Us?

MISS FOXHILL [*offstage*]: Mrs Holly? Mrs Holly?

MRS HOLLY: Somebody's callin' fo' me. Catharine, Gawge put it very badly but you know that it's TRUE WE DO HAVE TO GET WHAT SEBASTIAN HAS LEFT US IN HIS WILL, DEAREST! AND YOU WON'T LET US DOWN? PROMISE? YOU WON'T LET US DOWN?

GEORGE [*fiercely shouting*]: HERE COMES AUNT VI! Mama, Cathie, Aunt Violet's – here is Aunt Vi!

Scene Four

[MRS VENABLE *enters downstage area. Entrance music.*]

MRS HOLLY: *Cathie! Here's Aunt Vi!*

MRS VENABLE: She sees me and I see her. That's all that's necessary. Miss Foxhill, put my chair in this corner. Crank the back up a little.

[MISS FOXHILL *does this business.*]

More. More. Not that much! – Let it back down a little. All right. Now, then. I'll have my frozen daiquiri, now . . . Do any of you want coffee?

GEORGE: I'd like a chocolate malt.

MRS HOLLY: Gawge!

MRS VENABLE: This isn't a drugstore.

MRS HOLLY: Oh, Gawge is just being Gawge.

MRS VENABLE: That's what I *thought* he was being!

[*An uncomfortable silence falls.* MISS FOXHILL *creeps out like a burglar. She speaks in a breathless whisper, presenting a cardboard folder to* MRS VENABLE.]

MISS FOXHILL: Here's the portfolio marked Cabeza de Lobo. It has all your correspondence with the police there and the American Consul.

MRS VENABLE: I asked for the *English transcript*! It's in a separate –

MISS FOXHILL: Separate, yes, here it is!

MRS VENABLE: Oh . . .

MISS FOXHILL: And here's the report of the private investigators and here's the report of –

27

MRS VENABLE: Yes, yes, yes! Where's the Doctor?

MISS FOXHILL: On the phone in the library!

MRS VENABLE: Why does he choose such a moment to make a phone call?

MISS FOXHILL: He didn't make a phone call. He received a phone call from –

MRS VENABLE: Miss Foxhill, why are you talking to me like a burglar?!

[MISS FOXHILL *giggles a little desperately.*]

CATHARINE: Aunt Violet, she's frightened. – Can I move? Can I get up and move around till it starts?

MRS HOLLY: Cathie, Cathie, dear, did Gawge tell you that he received bids from every good fraternity on the Tulane campus and went Phi Delt because Paul Junior did?

MRS VENABLE: I see that he had the natural tact and good taste to come here this afternoon outfitted from head to foot in clothes that belonged to my son!

GEORGE: You gave 'em to me, Aunt Vi.

MRS VENABLE: I didn't know you'd parade them in front of me, George.

MRS HOLLY [*quickly*]: Gawge, tell Aunt Violet how grateful you are for –

GEORGE: I found a little Jew tailor on Britannia Street that makes alterations so good you'd never guess that they weren't cut *out* for me to *begin* with!

MRS HOLLY: And so reasonable! – Luckily, since it seems that Sebastian's wonderful, wonderful bequest to Gawge an' Cathie is going to be tied up a while!?

GEORGE: Aunt Vi? About the will?

[MRS HOLLY *coughs.*]

I was wondering if we can't figure out some way to, to –

MRS HOLLY: Gawge means to EXPEDITE it! To get through the red tape quicker?

MRS VENABLE: I understand his meaning. Foxhill, get the Doctor.

[*She has risen with her cane and hobbled to the door.*]

MISS FOXHILL [*exits calling*]: Doctor!

MRS HOLLY: Gawge, no more about money.

GEORGE: How do we know we'll ever see her again?

[CATHARINE *gasps and rises; she moves downstage, followed quickly by* SISTER FELICITY.]

SISTER [*mechanically*]: What's wrong, dear?

CATHARINE: I think I'm just dreaming this, it doesn't seem real!

MISS FOXHILL [*comes back out*]: He had to answer an urgent call from Lion's View.

[*Slight, tense pause.*]

MRS HOLLY: Violet! *Not* Lion's View!

[SISTER FELICITY *had started conducting* CATHARINE *back to the patio; she stops her now.*]

SISTER: Wait, dear.

CATHARINE: What for? I know what's coming.

MRS VENABLE [*at same time*]: Why? Are you all prepared to put out a thousand a month plus extra charges for treatments to keep the girl at St Mary's?

MRS HOLLY: Cathie? Cathie, dear?

[CATHARINE *has returned with the* SISTER.]

Tell Aunt Violet how grateful you are for her makin' it possible for you to rest an' recuperate at such a sweet, sweet place as St Mary's!

CATHARINE: No place for lunatics is a sweet, sweet place.

MRS HOLLY: But the food's good there. Isn't the food good there?

CATHARINE: Just give me written permission not to eat fried grits. I had yard privileges till I refused to eat fried grits.

SISTER: She lost yard privileges because she couldn't be trusted in the yard without constant supervision or even with it because she'd run to the fence and make signs to cars on the highway.

CATHARINE: Yes, I did, I did that because I've been trying for weeks to get a message out of that 'sweet, sweet place'.

MRS HOLLY: What message, dear?

CATHARINE: I got panicky, Mother.

MRS HOLLY: Sister, I don't understand.

GEORGE: What're you scared of, Sister?

CATHARINE: What they might do to me now, after they've done all the rest! – That man in the window's a specialist from Lion's View! We get newspapers. I know what they're . . .

[*The* DOCTOR *comes out.*]

MRS VENABLE: Why, Doctor, I thought you'd left us with just that little black bag to remember you by!

DOCTOR: Oh, no. Don't you remember our talk? I had to answer a call about a patient that –

MRS VENABLE: This is Dr Cukrowicz. He says it means 'sugar' and we can call him 'Sugar' –

[GEORGE *laughs.*]

He's a specialist from Lion's View.

CATHARINE [*cutting in*]: WHAT DOES HE SPECIALIZE IN?

MRS VENABLE: Something new. When other treatments have failed.

[*Pause. The jungle clamour comes up and subsides again.*]

CATHARINE: *Do you want to bore a hole in my skull and turn a knife in my brain?* Everything else was done to me!

[MRS HOLLY *sobs.* GEORGE *raps his knee with the tennis racket.*]

You'd have to have my mother's permission for that.

MRS VENABLE: I'm paying to keep you in a private asylum.

CATHARINE: You're not my legal guardian.

MRS VENABLE: Your mother's dependent on me. All of you are! – Financially . . .

CATHARINE: I think the situation is – clear to me, now . . .

MRS VENABLE: Good! In that case . . .

DOCTOR: I think a quiet atmosphere will get us the best results.

MRS VENABLE: I don't know what you mean by a quiet atmosphere.
She shouted, I didn't.

DOCTOR: Mrs Venable, let's try to keep things on a quiet level, now.
Your niece seems to be disturbed.

MRS VENABLE: She has every reason to be. She took my son from me,
and then she –

CATHARINE: Aunt Violet, you're not being fair.

MRS VENABLE: Oh, aren't I?

CATHARINE [*to the others*]: She's not being fair. [*Then back to* MRS VEN-
ABLE] Aunt Violet, you know why Sebastian asked me to travel
with him.

MRS VENABLE: Yes, I *do* know why!

CATHARINE: You weren't able to travel. You'd had a – [*She stops short.*]

MRS VENABLE: Go on! *What* had I had? Are you afraid to say it in
front of the Doctor? She meant that I had a stroke. – I DID NOT
HAVE A STROKE! – I had a slight aneurism. You know what that is,
Doctor? A little vascular convulsion! Not a haemorrhage, just a
little convulsion of a blood-vessel. I had it when I discovered that
she was trying to take my son away from me. Then I had it. It
gave a little temporary – muscular – contraction. – To one side of
my face. . . . [*She crosses back into main acting area.*] These people
are not blood-relatives of mine, they're my dead husband's relations. I always detested these people, my dead husband's sister
and – her two worthless children. But I did more than my duty to
keep their heads above water. To please my son, whose weakness
was being excessively softhearted, I went to the expense and
humiliation, yes, public humiliation, of giving this girl a début
which was a fiasco. Nobody liked her when I brought her out.
Oh, she had some kind of – notoriety! She had a sharp tongue
that some people mistook for wit. A habit of laughing in the faces
of decent people which would infuriate them, and also reflected
adversely on me and Sebastian, too. But, he, Sebastian, was
amused by this girl. While I was disgusted, sickened. And halfway
through the season, she was dropped off the party lists, yes,
dropped off the lists in spite of my position. Why? Because she'd
lost her head over a young married man, made a scandalous scene

at a Mardi Gras ball, in the middle of the ballroom. Then everybody dropped her like a hot – rock, but – [*She loses her breath.*] My son, Sebastian, still felt sorry for her and took her with him last summer instead of me . . .

CATHARINE [*springing up with a cry*]: I can't change truth. I'm not God! I'm not even sure that He could, I don't think God can change truth! How can I change the story of what happened to her son in Cabeza de Lobo?

MRS VENABLE [*at the same time*]: She was in love with my son!

CATHARINE [*overlapping*]: Let me go back to St Mary's. Sister Felicity, let's go back to Saint –

MRS VENABLE [*overlapping*]: Oh, no! That's not where you'll go!

CATHARINE [*overlapping*]: All right. *Lion's View*, but don't ask me to –

MRS VENABLE [*overlapping*]: You *know* that you were!

CATHARINE [*overlapping*]: That I was *what*, Aunt Violet?

MRS VENABLE [*overlapping*]: Don't call me 'Aunt'. You're the niece of my dead husband, not me!

MRS HOLLY [*overlapping*]: Catharine, Catharine, don't upset your – Doctor? Oh, Doctor!

[*But the* DOCTOR *is calmly observing the scene with detachment. The jungle garden is loud with the sounds of its feathered and scaled inhabitants.*]

CATHARINE: I don't want to, I didn't want to come here! I know what she thinks, she thinks I murdered her son, she thinks that I was responsible for his death.

MRS VENABLE: That's right. I told him when he told me that he was going with you in my place last summer that I'd never see him again and I never did. And only you know why!

CATHARINE: Oh, my God, I –

[*She rushes out toward garden, followed immediately by the* SISTER.]

SISTER: Miss Catharine, Miss Catharine –

DOCTOR [*overlapping*]: Mrs Venable?

SISTER [*overlapping*]: Miss Catharine?

DOCTOR [*overlapping*]: Mrs Venable?

MRS VENABLE: What?

DOCTOR: I'd like to be left alone with Miss Catharine for a few minutes.

MRS HOLLY: George, talk to her, George.

[GEORGE *crouches appealingly before the old lady's chair, peering close into her face, a hand on her knee.*]

GEORGE: Aunt Vi? Cathie can't go to Lion's View. Everyone in the Garden District would know you'd put your niece in a state asylum, Aunt Vi.

MRS VENABLE: Foxhill!

GEORGE: What do you want, Aunt Vi?

MRS VENABLE: Let go of my chair. Foxhill? Get me away from people!

GEORGE: Aunt Vi, listen, think of the talk it –

MRS VENABLE: I can't get up! Push me, push me away!

GEORGE [*rising, but holding chair*]: I'll push her, Miss Foxhill.

MRS VENABLE: Let go of my chair or –

MISS FOXHILL: Mr Holly, I –

GEORGE: I got to talk to her.

[*He pushes her chair downstage.*]

MRS VENABLE: Foxhill!

MISS FOXHILL: Mr Holly, she doesn't want you to push her.

GEORGE: I know what I'm doing. Leave me alone with Aunt Vi!

MRS VENABLE: Let go me or I'll *strike* you!

GEORGE: Oh, Aunt Vi!

MRS VENABLE: Foxhill!

MRS HOLLY: George –

GEORGE: Aunt Vi?

[*She strikes at him with her cane. He releases the chair and* MISS FOXHILL *pushes her off. He trots after her a few steps, then he returns to* MRS HOLLY, *who is sobbing into a handkerchief. He sighs, and sits down beside her, taking her hand. The scene fades as light is brought up on* CATHARINE *and the* SISTER *in the garden. The* DOCTOR *comes up to them.* MRS HOLLY *stretches her arms out to*]

GEORGE, *sobbing, and he crouches before her chair and rests his head in her lap. She strokes his head. During this: the* SISTER *has stood beside* CATHARINE, *holding on to her arm.*]

CATHARINE: You don't have to hold on to me. I can't run away.

DOCTOR: Miss Catharine?

CATHARINE: What?

DOCTOR: Your aunt is a very sick woman. She had a stroke last spring?

CATHARINE: Yes, she did, but she'll never admit it . . .

DOCTOR: You have to understand why.

CATHARINE: I do. I understand why. I didn't want to come here.

DOCTOR: Miss Catharine, do you hate her?

CATHARINE: I don't understand what hate is. How can you hate anybody and still be sane? You see, I still think I'm sane!

DOCTOR: You think she did have a stroke?

CATHARINE: She had a slight stroke in April. It just affected one side, the left side, of her face . . . but it was disfiguring and, after that, Sebastian couldn't use her.

DOCTOR: Use her? Did you say use her?

[*The sounds of the jungle garden are not loud but ominous.*]

CATHARINE: Yes, we all use each other and that's what we think of as love, and not being able to use each other is what's – *hate* . . .

DOCTOR: Do you hate her, Miss Catharine?

CATHARINE: Didn't you ask me that, once? And didn't I say that I didn't understand hate. A ship struck an iceberg at sea – everyone sinking –

DOCTOR: Go on, Miss Catharine!

CATHARINE: But that's no reason for everyone drowning for hating everyone drowning! Is it, Doctor?

DOCTOR: Tell me: what was your feeling for your cousin Sebastian?

CATHARINE: He liked me and so I loved him.

DOCTOR: In what way did you love him?

CATHARINE: The only way he'd accept: – a sort of motherly way. I tried to save him, Doctor.

DOCTOR: From what? Save him from what?

CATHARINE: Completing! – sort of! – *image*! – he had of himself as a
sort of! – *sacrifice* to a! – *terrible* sort of a –

DOCTOR: – God?

CATHARINE: Yes, a – *cruel* one, Doctor!

DOCTOR: How did you feel about that?

CATHARINE: Doctor, my feelings are the sort of feelings that you
have in a dream . . .

DOCTOR: Your life doesn't seem real to you?

CATHARINE: Suddenly last winter I began to write my journal in the
third person.

[*He graps her elbow and leads her out upon forestage. At the same
time* MISS FOXHILL *wheels* MRS VENABLE *off,* MRS HOLLY *weeps
into a handkerchief, and* GEORGE *rises and shrugs and turns his
back to the audience.*]

DOCTOR: Something happened last winter?

CATHARINE: At a Mardi Gras ball some – some boy that took me to
it got too drunk to stand up! [*A short, mirthless note of laughter.*] I
wanted to go home. My coat was in the cloakroom, they couldn't
find the check for it in his pockets. I said, 'Oh, hell, let it go!' – I
started out for a taxi. Somebody took my arm and said, 'I'll drive
you home.' He took off his coat as we left the hotel and put it over
my shoulders, and then I looked at him and – I don't think I'd ever
even seen him before then, really! – He took me home in his car,
but took me another place first. We stopped near the Duelling
Oaks at the end of Esplanade Street . . . Stopped! – I said, 'What
for?' – He didn't answer, just struck a match in the car to light a
cigarette in the car and I looked at him in the car and I knew 'what
for'! – I think I got out of the car before he got out of the car, and
we walked through the wet grass to the great misty oaks as if
somebody was calling us for help there!

[*Pause. The subdued, toneless bird-cries in the garden turn to a single
bird-song.*]

DOCTOR: After that?

CATHARINE: I lost him. – He took me home and said an awful thing to me. 'We'd better forget it,' he said, 'my wife's expecting a child and –' – I just entered the house and sat there thinking a little and then I suddenly called a taxi and went right back to the Roosevelt Hotel ballroom. The ball was still going on. I thought I'd gone back to pick up my borrowed coat, but that wasn't what I'd gone back for. I'd gone back to make a scene on the floor of the ballroom, yes, I didn't stop at the cloakroom to pick up Aunt Violet's old mink stole, no, I rushed right into the ballroom and spotted him on the floor and ran up to him and beat him as hard as I could in the face and chest with my fists till – Cousin Sebastian took me away. – After that, the next morning, I started writing my diary in the third person, singular, such as 'She's still living this morning', meaning that *I* was . . . 'WHAT'S NEXT FOR HER? GOD KNOWS!' – I couldn't go out any more. – However, one morning my Cousin Sebastian came in my bedroom and said: 'Get up!' – Well . . . if you're still alive after dying, well then, you're obedient, Doctor. – I got up. He took me downtown to a place for passport photos. Said: 'Mother can't go abroad with me this summer. You're going to go with me this summer instead of Mother.' – If you don't believe me, read my journal of Paris! – 'She woke up at daybreak this morning, had her coffee, and dressed and took a brief walk –'

DOCTOR: *Who* did?

CATHARINE: *She* did. *I* did – from the Hotel Plaza Athénée to the Place de l'Étoile as if pursued by a pack of Siberian wolves! [*She laughs her tired, helpless laugh.*] – Went right through all stop signs – couldn't wait for green signals. – 'Where did she think she was going? Back to the Duelling Oaks?' – Everything chilly and dim but his hot, ravenous mouth! on –

DOCTOR: Miss Catharine, let me give you something.

[*The others go out, leaving* CATHARINE *and the* DOCTOR *onstage.*]

CATHARINE: Do I have to have the injection again, this time? What am I going to be stuck with this time, Doctor? I don't care. I've been stuck so often that if you connected me with a garden hose I'd make a good sprinkler.

DOCTOR [*preparing needle*]: Please take off your jacket.

[*She does. The* DOCTOR *gives her an injection.*]

CATHARINE: I didn't feel it.
DOCTOR: That's good. Now sit down.

[*She sits down.*]

CATHARINE: Shall I start counting backwards from a hundred?
DOCTOR: Do you like counting backwards?
CATHARINE: Love it! Just love it! One hundred! Ninety-nine! Ninety-eight! Ninety-seven! Ninety-six. Ninety – five – Oh! – I already feel it! How funny!
DOCTOR: That's right. Close your eyes for a minute.

[*He moves his chair closer to hers. Half a minute passes.*]

Miss Catharine? I want you to give me something.
CATHARINE: Name it and it's yours, Doctor Sugar.
DOCTOR: Give me all your resistance.
CATHARINE: Resistance to what?
DOCTOR: The truth. Which you're going to tell me.
CATHARINE: The truth's the one thing I have never resisted!
DOCTOR: Sometimes people just think they don't resist it, but still do.
CATHARINE: They say it's at the bottom of a bottomless well, you know.
DOCTOR: Relax.
CATHARINE: Truth.
DOCTOR: Don't talk.
CATHARINE: Where was I, now? At ninety?
DOCTOR: You don't have to count backwards.
CATHARINE: At ninety something?
DOCTOR: You can open your eyes.
CATHARINE: Oh, I do feel funny!

[*Silence, pause.*]

You know what I think you're doing? I think you're trying to hypnotize me. Aren't you? You're looking so straight at me and doing something to me with your eyes and your – eyes . . . Is that what you're doing to me?

DOCTOR: Is that what you *feel* I'm doing?

CATHARINE: Yes! I feel so peculiar. And it's not just the drug.

DOCTOR: Give me all your resistance. See. I'm holding my hand out. I want you to put yours in mine and give me all your resistance. Pass all of your resistance out of your hand to mine.

CATHARINE: Here's my hand. But there's no resistance in it.

DOCTOR: You are totally passive.

CATHARINE: Yes, I am.

DOCTOR: You will do what I ask.

CATHARINE: Yes, I will try.

DOCTOR: You will tell the true story.

CATHARINE: Yes, I will.

DOCTOR: The absolutely true story. No lies, nothing not spoken. Everything told, exactly.

CATHARINE: Everything. Exactly. Because I'll have to. Can I – can I stand up?

DOCTOR: Yes, but be careful. You might feel a little bit dizzy.

[*She struggles to rise, then falls back.*]

CATHARINE: I can't get up! Tell me to. Then I think I could do it.

DOCTOR: Stand up.

[*She rises unsteadily.*]

CATHARINE: How funny! Now I can! Oh, I do feel dizzy! Help me, I'm –

[*He rushes to support her.*]

– about to fall over . . .

[*He holds her. She looks out vaguely toward the brilliant, steaming garden. Looks back at him. Suddenly sways toward him, against him.*]

DOCTOR: You see, you lost your balance.

CATHARINE: No, I didn't. I did what I wanted to do without you telling me to. [*She holds him tight against her.*] Let me! Let! Let! Let me! Let me, let me, oh, let me . . . [*She crushes her mouth to his violently. He tries to disengage himself. She presses her lips to his fiercely, clutching his body against her. Her brother* GEORGE *enters.*] Please hold me! I've been so lonely. It's lonelier than death, if I've gone mad, it's lonelier than death!

GEORGE [*shocked, disgusted*]: *Cathie!* – you've got a hell of a nerve.

[*She falls back, panting, covers her face, runs a few paces and grabs the back of a chair.* MRS HOLLY *enters.*]

MRS HOLLY: What's the matter, George? Is Catharine ill?

GEORGE: No.

DOCTOR: Miss Catharine had an injection that made her a little unsteady.

MRS HOLLY: What did he say about Catharine?

[CATHARINE *has gone out into the dazzling jungle of the garden.*]

SISTER [*returning*]: She's gone into the garden.

DOCTOR: That's all right. She'll come back when I call her.

SISTER: It may be all right for you. You're not responsible for her.

[MRS VENABLE *has re-entered.*]

MRS VENABLE: Call her now!

DOCTOR: Miss Catharine! Come back. [*To the* SISTER] Bring her back, please, Sister!

[CATHARINE *enters quietly, a little unsteady.*]

Now, Miss Catharine, you're going to tell the true story.

CATHARINE: Where do I start the story?

DOCTOR: Wherever you think it started.

CATHARINE: I think it started the day he was born in this house.

MRS VENABLE: Ha! You see!

GEORGE: Cathie.

DOCTOR: Let's start later than that.

[*Pause.*]

Shall we begin with last summer?

CATHARINE: Oh. Last summer.

DOCTOR: Yes. Last summer.

[*There is a long pause. The raucous sounds in the garden fade into a bird-song which is clear and sweet.* MRS HOLLY *coughs.* MRS VENABLE *stirs impatiently.* GEORGE *crosses downstage to catch* CATHARINE's *eye as he lights a cigarette.*]

CATHARINE: Could I –?

MRS VENABLE: Keep that boy away from her!

GEORGE: She wants to smoke, Aunt Vi.

CATHARINE: Something helps in the – hands . . .

SISTER: Unh unh!

DOCTOR: It's all right, Sister. [*He lights her cigarette.*] About last summer: how did it begin?

CATHARINE: It began with his kindness and the six days at sea that took me so far away from the – Duelling Oaks that I forgot them, nearly. He was affectionate with me, so sweet and attentive to me, that some people took us for a honeymoon couple until they noticed that we had – separate state-rooms, and – then in Paris, he took me to Patou and Schiaparelli's – *this* is from Schiaparelli's! [*Like a child, she indicates her suit.*] – bought me so many new clothes that I gave away my old ones to make room for my new ones in my new luggage to – travel . . . I turned into a peacock! Of course, so was *he* one, too . . .

GEORGE: *Ha ha!*

MRS VENABLE: Shh!

CATHARINE: But then I made the mistake of responding too much to his kindness, of taking hold of his hand before he'd take hold of mine, of holding on to his arm and leaning on his shoulder, of appreciating his kindness more than he wanted me to, and, suddenly last summer, he began to be restless, and – oh!

DOCTOR: Go on.

CATHARINE: The Blue Jay notebook!

DOCTOR: Did you say notebook?

MRS VENABLE: I know what she means by that. She's talking about the school composition book with a Blue Jay trademark that

Sebastian used for making notes and revisions on his 'Poem of Summer'. It went with him everywhere that he went, in his jacket pocket, even his dinner jacket. I have the one that he had with him last summer. *Foxhill! The Blue Jay notebook!*

[MISS FOXHILL *rushes in with a gasp.*]

It came with his personal effects shipped back from Cabeza de Lobo.

DOCTOR: I don't quite get the connexion between new clothes and so forth and the Blue Jay notebook.

MRS VENABLE: I HAVE IT! – Doctor, tell her I've found it.

[MISS FOXHILL *hears this as she comes back out of house: gasps with relief, retires.*]

DOCTOR: With all these interruptions it's going to be awfully hard to –

MRS VENABLE: This is important. I don't know why she mentioned the Blue Jay notebook, but I want you to see it. Here it is, here! [*She holds up a notebook and leafs swiftly through the pages.*] Title? 'Poem of Summer', and the date of the summer – 1935. After that: *what*? *Blank pages, blank pages*, nothing but *nothing*! – last summer . . .

DOCTOR: What's that got to do with – ?

MRS VENABLE: His destruction? I'll tell you. A poet's vocation is something that rests on something as thin and fine as the web of a spider, Doctor. That's all that holds him *over*! – out of destruction . . . Few, very few are able to do it alone! Great help is needed. I *did* give it! She *didn't*.

CATHARINE: She's right about that. I failed him. I wasn't able to keep the web from – breaking . . . I saw it breaking but couldn't save or – repair it!

MRS VENABLE: There now, the truth's coming out. We had an agreement between us, a sort of contract or covenant between us which he broke last summer when he broke away from me and took her with him, not me! When he was frightened and I knew when and what of, because his hands would shake and his eyes looked in, not out, I'd reach across a table and touch his hands and say not a word, just look, and touch his hands with my hand until his hands stopped shaking and his eyes looked out, not in, and in the morning, the poem would be continued. *Continued until it was finished!*

[*The following ten speeches are said very rapidly, overlapping.*]

CATHARINE: I – couldn't!

MRS VENABLE: *Naturally* not! He was *mine*! I *knew* how to help him, I *could*! You didn't, you couldn't!

DOCTOR: These interruptions –

MRS VENABLE: I would say 'You *will*' and he *would*, I – !

CATHARINE: Yes, you see, I failed him! And so, last summer, we went to Cabeza de Lobo, we flew down there from where he gave up writing his poem last summer . . .

MRS VENABLE: Because he'd broken our –

CATHARINE: Yes! Yes, something had broken, that string of pearls that old mothers hold their sons by like a – sort of a – sort of – *umbilical* cord, *long – after* . . .

MRS VENABLE: She means that I held him back from –

DOCTOR: *Please!*

MRS VENABLE: *Destruction!*

CATHARINE: All I know is that suddenly, last summer, he wasn't young any more, and we went to Cabeza de Lobo, and he suddenly switched from the evenings to the beach . . .

DOCTOR: From evenings? To beach?

CATHARINE: I mean from the evenings to the afternoons and from the fa – fash –

[*Silence.* MRS HOLLY *draws a long, long painful breath.* GEORGE *stirs impatiently.*]

DOCTOR: Fashionable! Is that the word you –?

CATHARINE: Yes. Suddenly, last summer Cousin Sebastian changed to the afternoons and the beach.

DOCTOR: What beach?

CATHARINE: In Cabeza de Lobo there is a beach that's named for Sebastian's name saint, it's known as La Playa San Sebastian, and that's where we started spending all afternoon, every day.

DOCTOR: What kind of beach was it?

CATHARINE: It was a big city beach near the harbour.

DOCTOR: It was a big public beach?

CATHARINE: Yes, public.

MRS VENABLE: It's little statements like that that give her away.

[*The* DOCTOR *rises and crosses to* MRS VENABLE *without breaking his concentration on* CATHARINE.]

After all I've told you about his fastidiousness, can you accept such a statement?

DOCTOR: You mustn't interrupt her.

MRS VENABLE [*overlapping him*]: That Sebastian would go every day to some dirty free public beach near a harbour? A man that had to go out a mile in a boat to find water fit to swim in?

DOCTOR: Mrs Venable, no matter what she says, you have to let her say it without any more interruptions or this interview will be useless.

MRS VENABLE: I won't speak again. I'll keep still, if it kills me.

CATHARINE: I don't want to go on . . .

DOCTOR: Go on with the story. Every afternoon last summer your Cousin Sebastian and you went out to this free public beach?

CATHARINE: No, it wasn't the free one, the free one was right next to it, there was a fence between the free beach and the one that we went to that charged a small charge of admission.

DOCTOR: Yes, and what did you do there?

[*He still stands besides* MRS VENABLE *and the light gradually changes as the girl gets deeper into her story: the light concentrates on* CATHARINE, *the other figures sink into shadow.*]

Did anything happen there that disturbed you about it?

CATHARINE: Yes!

DOCTOR: What?

CATHARINE: He bought me a swim-suit I didn't want to wear. I laughed. I said, 'I can't wear that. It's a scandal to the jaybirds!'

DOCTOR: What did you mean by that? That the suit was immodest?

CATHARINE: My God, yes! It was a one-piece suit made of white lisle, the water made it transparent! [*She laughs sadly at the memory of it.*] – I didn't want to swim in it, but he'd grab my hand and drag me into the water, all the way in, and I'd come out looking naked!

DOCTOR: Why did he do that? Did you understand why?

CATHARINE: Yes! To attract! – Attention.

DOCTOR: He wanted you to attract attention, did he, because he felt you were moody? Lonely? He wanted to shock you out of your depression last summer?

CATHARINE: Don't you understand? I was PROCURING for him!

[*MRS VENABLE's gasp is like the sound that a great hooked fish might make.*]

She used to do it, *too*.

[*MRS VENABLE cries out.*]

Not consciously! She didn't *know* that she was procuring for him in the smart, the fashionable places they used to go to before last summer! Sebastian was shy with people. She wasn't. Neither was I. We both did the same thing for him, made contacts for him, but she did it in nice places and in decent ways and I had to do it the way that I just told you! – Sebastian was lonely, Doctor, and the empty Blue Jay notebook got bigger and bigger, so big it was big and empty as that big empty blue sea and sky . . . I knew what I was doing. I came out in the French Quarter years before I came out in the Garden District . . .

MRS HOLLY: Oh, Cathie! Sister . . .

DOCTOR: Hush!

CATHARINE: And before long, when the weather got warmer and the beach so crowded, he didn't need me anymore for that purpose. The ones on the free beach began to climb over the fence or swim around it, bands of homeless young people that lived on the free beach like scavenger dogs, hungry children . . . So now he let me wear a decent dark suit. I'd go to a faraway empty end of the beach, write postcards and letters and keep up my – third-person

journal till it was – five o'clock and time to meet him outside the
bathhouses, on the street . . . He would come out, *followed.*

DOCTOR: Who would follow him out?

CATHARINE: The homeless, hungry young people that had climbed
over the fence from the free beach that they lived on. He'd pass
out tips among them as if they'd all – shined his shoes or called
taxis for him . . . Each day the crowd was bigger, noisier, greedier!
– Sebastian began to be frightened. – At last we stopped going out
there . . .

DOCTOR: And then? After that? After you quit going out to the public
beach?

CATHARINE: Then one day, a few days after we stopped going out to
the beach – it was one of those white blazing days in Cabeza de
Lobo, not a blazing hot *blue* one but a blazing hot *white* one.

DOCTOR: Yes?

CATHARINE: We had a late lunch at one of those open-air restaurants
on the sea there. – Sebastian was white as the weather. He had on
a spotless white silk Shantung suit and a white silk tie and a white
panama and white shoes, white – white lizard skin – pumps! He
– [*She throws back her head in a startled laugh at the recollection.*] –
kept touching his face and his throat here and there with a white
silk handkerchief and popping little white pills in his mouth, and
I knew he was having a bad time with his heart and was frightened about it and that was the reason we hadn't gone out to the
beach . . .

[*During the monologue the lights have changed, the surrounding area
has dimmed out and a hot white spot is focused on* CATHARINE.]

'I think we ought to go north,' he kept saying, 'I think we've done
Cabeza de Lobo, I think we've done it, don't you?' *I* thought we'd
done it! – but I had learned it was better not to seem to have an
opinion because if I did, well, Sebastian, well, you know Sebastian, he always preferred to do what no one else wanted to do,
and I always tried to give the impression that I was agreeing reluctantly to his wishes . . . it was a – game . . .

SISTER: She's dropped her cigarette.

DOCTOR: I've got it, Sister.

[*There are whispers, various movements in the penumbra. The* DOC-
TOR *fills a glass for her from the cocktail-shaker.*]

CATHARINE: Where was I? Oh, yes, that five o'clock lunch at one of
those fish-places along the harbour of Cabeza de Lobo, it was
between the city and the sea, and there were naked children along
the beach which was fenced off with barbed wire from the restaurant and we had our table less than a yard from the barbed-wire
fence that held the beggars at bay . . . There were naked children
along the beach, a band of frightfully thin and dark naked children that looked a flock of plucked birds, and they would come
darting up to the barbed-wire fence as if blown there by the wind,
the hot white wind from the sea, all crying out, '*Pan, pan, pan!*'

DOCTOR [*quietly*]: What's *pan?*

CATHARINE: The word for bread, and they made gobbling noises
with their little black mouths, stuffing their little black fists to
their mouths and making those gobbling noises, with frightful
grins! – Of course we were sorry that we had come to this place,
but it was too late to go . . .

DOCTOR [*quietly*]: Why was it 'too late to go'?

CATHARINE: I told you Cousin Sebastian wasn't well. He was popping those little white pills in his mouth. I think he had popped in
so many of them that they had made him feel weak . . . His, his!
– eyes looked – dazed, but he said: 'Don't look at those little mon-
sters. Beggars are a social disease in this country. If you look at
them, you get sick of the country, it spoils the whole country for
you . . .'

DOCTOR: Go on.

CATHARINE: I'm going on. I have to wait now and then till it gets
clearer. Under the drug it has to be a vision or nothing comes . . .

DOCTOR: All right?

CATHARINE: Always when I was with him I did what he told me. I
didn't look at the band of naked children, not even when the waiters drove them away from the barbed-wire fence with sticks! –
Rushing out through a wicket gate like an assault party in war!

– and beating them screaming away from the barbed-wire fence
with the sticks . . . Then!

[*Pause.*]

DOCTOR: Go on, Miss Catharine, what comes next in the vision?

CATHARINE: The, the the! – band of children began to – serenade
us . . .

DOCTOR: Do what?

CATHARINE: Play for us! On instruments! Make music! – if you could
call it music . . .

DOCTOR: Oh?

CATHARINE: Their, their – instruments were – instruments of percussion! – Do you know what I mean?

DOCTOR [*making a note*]: Yes. Instruments of percussion such as –
drums?

CATHARINE: I stole glances at them when Cousin Sebastian wasn't
looking, and as well as I could make out in the white blaze of the
sand-beach, the instruments were tin cans strung together.

DOCTOR [*slowly, writing*]: *Tin – cans – strung – together.*

CATHARINE: *And, and, and, and – and!* – bits of metal, *other* bits of
metal that had been flattened out, made into –

DOCTOR: What?

CATHARINE: *Cymbals!* You know? *Cymbals?*

DOCTOR: Yes. Brass plates hit together.

CATHARINE: That's right, Doctor. – Tin cans flattened out and
clashed together! – Cymbals . . .

DOCTOR: Yes. I understand. What's after that, in the vision?

CATHARINE [*rapidly, panting a little*]: And others had paper bags, bags
made out of – coarse paper! – with something on a string inside
the bags which they pulled up and down, back and forth, to make
a sort of a –

DOCTOR: Sort of a –?

CATHARINE: Noise like –

DOCTOR: Noise like?

CATHARINE [*rising stiffly from chair*]: Ooompa! Oompa! Ooooooompa!

DOCTOR: Ahhh . . . a sound like a *tuba?*

CATHARINE: That's right! – they made a sound like a tuba . . .

DOCTOR: Oompa, oompa, oompa, like a tuba.

[*He is making a note of the description.*]

CATHARINE: Oompa, oompa, oompa, like a –

[*Short pause.*]

DOCTOR: – Tuba . . .

CATHARINE: All during lunch they stayed at a – a fairly *close* – *distance* . . .

DOCTOR: Go on with the vision, Miss Catharine.

CATHARINE [*striding about the table*]: *Oh, I'm going on, nothing could stop it now!!*

DOCTOR: Your Cousin Sebastian was *entertained* by this – *concert*?

CATHARINE: I think he was *terrified* of it!

DOCTOR: Why was he terrified of it?

CATHARINE: I think he recognized some of the musicians, some of the boys, between childhood and – older . . .

DOCTOR: What did he do? Did he do anything about it, Miss Catharine? – Did he complain to the manager about it?

CATHARINE: *What* manager? *God*? Oh, no! – The manager of the fish-place on the beach? Ha ha! – No! – You don't understand my cousin!

DOCTOR: What do you mean?

CATHARINE: *He!* – *accepted!* – *all!* – as – how! – things! – are! – And thought nobody had any right to complain or interfere in any way whatsoever, and even though he knew that what was awful was awful, that what was wrong was wrong, and my Cousin Sebastian was certainly never sure that anything was wrong! – He thought it unfitting to ever take any action about anything whatsoever! – except to go on doing as something in him directed . . .

DOCTOR: What did something in him direct him to do? – I mean on this occasion in Cabeza de Lobo.

CATHARINE: After the salad, before they brought the coffee, he suddenly pushed himself away from the table, and said, 'They've got to stop that! Waiter, make them stop that. I'm not a well man, I have a heart condition, it's making me sick!' – This was the first time that Cousin Sebastian had ever attempted to correct a human situation! – I think perhaps that *that* was his – fatal error . . . It was then that the waiters, all eight or ten of them, charged out of the barbed-wire wicket gate and beat the little musicians away with clubs and skillets and anything hard that they could snatch from the kitchen! – Cousin Sebastian left the table. He stalked out of the restaurant after throwing a handful of paper money on the table and he fled from the place. I followed. It was all white outside. White hot, a blazing white hot, hot blazing white, at five o'clock in the afternoon in the city of – Cabeza de Lobo. It looked as if –

DOCTOR: It looked as if?

CATHARINE: As if a huge white bone had caught on fire in the sky and blazed so bright it was white and turned the sky and everything under the sky white with it!

DOCTOR: White . . .

CATHARINE: Yes – white . . .

DOCTOR: You followed your Cousin Sebastian out of the restaurant on to the hot white street?

CATHARINE: Running up and down hill . . .

DOCTOR: You ran up and down hill?

CATHARINE: No, no! *Didn't* – move either *way*! – at first, we were –

[*During this recitation there are various sound effects. The percussive sounds described are very softly employed.*]

I rarely made any suggestion, but *this* time I *did*. . . .

DOCTOR: What did you suggest?

CATHARINE: Cousin Sebastian seemed to be paralysed near the entrance of the café, so I said, 'Let's go.' I remember that it was a very wide and steep white street, and I said, 'Cousin Sebastian, down that way is the waterfront and we are more likely to find a taxi near there . . . Or why don't we go back in? – and have them *call* us a taxi! Oh, let's do! Let's do *that*, that's better!' And he said, '*Mad*, are you *mad*? Go back in that filthy place? Never! That gang of kids shouted vile things about me to the waiters!' 'Oh,' I said, 'then let's go down toward the docks, down there at the bottom of the hill, let's not try to climb the hill in this dreadful heat.' And Cousin Sebastian shouted, 'Please shut up, let me handle this situation, will you? I want to handle this thing.' And he started up the steep street with a hand stuck in his jacket where I knew he was having a pain in his chest from his palpitations . . . But he walked faster and faster, in panic, but the faster he walked the louder and closer it got!

DOCTOR: What got louder?

CATHARINE: The music.

DOCTOR: The music again.

CATHARINE: The oompa-oompa of the – following band. – They'd somehow gotten through the barbed wire and out on the street, and they were following, following! – up the blazing white street. The band of naked children pursued us up the steep white street in the sun that was like a great white bone of a giant beast that had caught on fire in the sky! – Sebastian started to run and they all screamed at once and seemed to fly in the air, they outran him so quickly. I screamed. I heard Sebastian scream, he screamed just once before this flock of black plucked little birds that pursued him and overtook him halfway up the white hill.

DOCTOR: And you, Miss Catharine, what did *you* do, then?

CATHARINE: Ran!

DOCTOR: Ran where?

CATHARINE: Down! Oh, I ran down, the easier direction to run was down, down, down, down! – The hot, white, blazing street, screaming out 'Help' all the way, till –

DOCTOR: What?

CATHARINE: – Waiters, police, and others – ran out of buildings and rushed back up the hill with me. When we got back to where my Cousin Sebastian had disappeared in the flock of featherless little black sparrows, he – he was lying naked as they had been naked against a white wall, and this you won't believe, nobody *has* believed it, nobody *could* believe it, nobody, nobody on earth could possibly believe it, and I don't *blame* them! – They had *devoured* parts of him.

[MRS VENABLE *cries out softly.*]

Torn or cut parts of him away with their hands or knives or maybe those jagged tin cans they made music with, they had torns bits of him away and stuffed them into those gobbling fierce little empty black mouths of theirs. There wasn't a sound any more, there was nothing to see but Sebastian, what was left of him, that looked like a big white-paper-wrapped bunch of red roses had been *torn, thrown, crushed!* – against that blazing white wall . . .

[MRS VENABLE *springs with amazing power from her wheelchair, stumbles erratically but swiftly toward the girl and tries to strike her with her cane. The* DOCTOR *snatches it from her and catches her as she is about to fall. She gasps hoarsely several times as he leads her toward the exit.*]

MRS VENABLE [*offstage*]: *Lion's View! State asylum, cut this hideous story out of her brain!*

[MRS HOLLY *sobs and crosses to* GEORGE, *who turns away from her.*]

GEORGE: Mom, I'll quit school, I'll get a job, I'll –
MRS HOLLY: Hush, son! Doctor, can't you say something?

[*Pause. The* DOCTOR *comes downstage.* CATHARINE *wanders out into the garden, followed by the* SISTER.]

DOCTOR [*after a while, reflectively, into space*]: I think we ought at least to consider the possibility that the girl's story could be true . . .

The Milk Train Doesn't Stop Here Anymore

Author's Notes

Sometimes theatrical effects and devices such as those I have adopted in the third (and I hope final) version of this play are ascribed to affectation or 'artiness', so it may be helpful for me to explain a bit of my intention in the use of these effects and devices, and let the play's production justify or condemn them.

I have added to the cast a pair of stage assistants that function in a way that's between the Kabuki Theatre of Japan and the chorus of Greek theatre. My excuse, or reason, is that I think the play will come off better the further it is removed from conventional theatre since it's been rightly described as an allegory and as a 'sophisticated fairy-tale'.

Stage assistants in Japanese Kabuki are a theatrical expedient. They work on-stage during the performance, shifting set-pieces, placing and removing properties and furniture. Now and then in this play they have lines to speak, very short ones that serve as cues to the principal performers ... They should be regarded, therefore, as members of the cast. They sometimes take a balletic part in the action of the play. They should be dressed in black, very simply, to represent invisibility to the other players. The other players should never appear to see them, even when they speak or take part in the action, except when they appear 'in costume'.

The setting represents the library and bedroom of the white villa, downstage, and the bedrooms of the pink and blue villinos: most importantly, the terrace of the white villa, which I think should extend the whole width of the proscenium with a small apron for a white iron bench, a step down from the terrace.

Separations between interior and exterior should not be clearly defined except by lighting. When a single interior is being used, the other interior areas should be masked by light, folding screens, painted to blend with the cyclorama, that is, in sea-and-sky colours: they should be set in place and removed by the stage assistants. The cyclorama and these folding screens represent, preferably in a semi-abstract style, the mountain-sea-sky of Italy's 'Divina Costiera' in summer.

Since the villas are, naturally, much further apart than they can appear on the stage, the director could adopt a convention of having actors, going from one villa to another, make their exits into the wings: wait till the stage assistants have removed the screens that mask the next interior to be used: then come back out and enter that area.

August 1963

Prologue

At rise: the STAGE ASSISTANTS *are onstage: All the interior areas are masked by their individual screens: the light on the cyclorama suggests early dawn.*

ONE: Daybreak: flag-raising ceremony on Mrs Goforth's mountain.

TWO: Above the oldest sea in the Western world.

ONE: Banner.

> [TWO *hands it to him.* TWO *places the staff in a socket near the right wings and attaches the flag to it. A fan in the wings whips it out as it is being raised so that the audience can see the device on it clearly.*]

ONE: The device on the banner is a golden griffin.

TWO: A mythological monster, half lion and half eagle.

ONE: And completely human.

TWO: Yes, wholly and completely human, that's true.

ONE: We are also a device.

TWO: A theatrical device of ancient and oriental origin.

ONE: With occidental variations, however.

TOGETHER: We are Stage Assistants. We move the screens that mask the interior playing areas of the stage presentation.

ONE: We fetch and carry.

TWO: Furniture and props.

ONE: To make the presentation – the play or masque or pageant – move more gracefully quickly through the course of the two final days of Mrs Goforth's existence.

MRS GOFORTH'S VOICE [*off, half-sleeping*]: AHHHHHHHH, MEEEEEEEEE . . .

[*The* HARMONIUM PLAYER *produces a sound of distant church bells.*]

ONE: The actors will not seem to hear us except when we're in costume.

TWO: They will never see us, except when we're in costume.

ONE: Sometimes we will give them cues for speech and participate in the action.

MRS GOFORTH'S VOICE [*off*]: AHHHHHH, AHHHHHH, AHHHHHH . . .

[THEY *show no reaction to this human cry.*]

MRS GOFORTH'S VOICE [*off, more wakefully*]: ANOTHER DAY, OH, CHRIST, OH, MOTHER OF CHRIST!

[*There is silence, a pause, as the cyclorama's lighting indicates the progress of the day toward the meridian.*]

TOGETHER: Our hearts are invisible, too.

[*The fan that whipped out the flag bearing the personal emblem, the griffin, of* MRS GOFORTH, *dies down and the flag subsides with it and will not whip out again till the flag-lowering ceremony which will take place near the end of the play.*

Now it is Noon. Electric buzzers sound from various points on the stage. The STAGE ASSISTANTS *cross rapidly up centre and remove a screen, the middle panel of which is topped by* MRS GOFORTH'S *heraldic device, the gold griffin. The library of the white villa is unmasked and the play begins.*]

Scene One

MRS GOFORTH *and her secretary*, BLACKIE.

MRS GOFORTH: I made my greatest mistake when I put a fast car in
his hands, that red demon sports car, his fighting cock, I called it,
which he drove insanely, recklessly, between my estate and the
Casino at Monte Carlo, so recklessly that the police commissioner
of Monaco came personally to ask me. Correction, *beg* me. Correction, *implore* me! – To insist that he go with me in the Rolls
with a chauffeur at the wheel, as a protection of his life and of the
lives of others. – M. Le Commissionaire, I said, for me there are
no others. – I know, Madame, he said, but for the others there
are others. – Then I confessed to the Commissioner of Police that
over this young poet with Romanov blood in his veins, I had no
more control than my hands had over the sea-wind or the storms
of the sea. At night he had flying dreams, he would thrash his
arms like wings, and once his hand on which he wore a signet ring
with the heavy Romanov crest struck me in the mouth and drew
blood. After *that, necessarily – twin beds* . . .

BLACKIE: Mrs Goforth, excuse me, but the last thing I have typed up
is – oh, here it is. – 'My first two husbands were ugly as apes and
my third one resembled an ostrich.' – Now if this passage you're
dictating to me comes in direct sequence it will sound as if you
had put the fast car in the hands of the ostrich.

[*A long, tempestuous pause.*]

MRS GOFORTH: Aren't you the sly one, oh, you're sly as ten flies when
you want to give me the needle, aren't you, Miss Blackie? My first

three marriages were into Dun and Bradstreet's, and the Social Register, both! – My first husband, Harlon Goforth, whose name I still carry after three later marriages – that dignified financier, TYCOON! – was a man that Presidents put next to their wives at banquets in the White House, and you sit there smoking in my face, when you know I've been told to quit smoking, and you make a joke of my work with a dead-pan expression on your Vassar-girl face, in your Vassar-girl voice, and *I WILL NOT TOLERATE IT!* – You know goddam well. I'm talking about my *fourth* husband, the *last* one, the one I married for love, who plunged off the Grande Corniche between Monte Carlo and – died that night in my arms in a clinic at Nice: and my heart died with him! Forever.

[*Her voice breaks.*]

BLACKIE: I'm sorry, Mrs Goforth. [*Puts out cigarette.*] – I'm no writer but I do think in writing there has to be some kind of logical – sequence, continuity – between one bit and the next bit, and the last thing you dictated to me –

MRS GOFORTH: Was it something I put on the tape-recorder in my bedroom after I'd been given one of those injections that upset my balance at night?

BLACKIE: I took it off your bedroom tape this morning.

MRS GOFORTH: Always check those night recordings with me before we begin to work the following morning. We're working against time, Blackie. Remember, try to remember, I've got two dead-lines to meet, my New York publishers and my London publishers, both, have my memoirs on their Fall List. I said Fall. It's already late in August. Now do you see why there's no time for goofing or must I draw you a picture of autumn leaves falling?

BLACKIE: Mrs Goforth, I think those publishers' dead-lines are un-realistic, not to say cruel, and as for me, I not only have to function as a secretary but as an *editor*, I have to *collate* the material you dictate to me and I'm not being sly or cruel, I'm just being *honest* with you when I tell you –

MRS GOFORTH [*cutting in*]: All cruel people describe themselves as paragons of frankness!

BLACKIE: I think we'd better stop now.

MRS GOFORTH: I think we'd better go *on*, now!

BLACKIE: Mrs Goforth, the Police Commissioner of Monaco was right when he told you that there were 'others'. I am one of those 'others'. I've had no sleep, scarcely any at all and –

MRS GOFORTH: *You've* had no sleep? What about me, how much sleep do *I* get?

BLACKIE: You sleep till noon or after!

MRS GOFORTH: Under sedation, with nightmares!

BLACKIE: – Your broker is on the phone . . .

[The STAGE ASSISTANTS *have entered with phone.*]

MRS GOFORTH [*immediately brightening*]: Chuck, baby, how're we doing? Ah-huh, glamour stocks still slipping? Don't hold on to 'em, dump them before they drop under what I bought 'em at, baby. We'll start buying back when they hit the basement level. – Don't give me an argument, SELL! *SELL! HELL!* – It's building into a crash! So, baby, I'm hitting the silk! High, low, Jack and the game! Ho ho!

[*She bangs down the phone, exhilarated, and it is removed by one of the* STAGE ASSISTANTS. *The other* ASSISTANT *has rushed to the stage right wings and he now appears in a white doctor's jacket. This is one of the costumes that make the assistants seen and heard by the other actors.*]

ASSISTANT (*as* DR LULLO): *Buon' giorno!*

MRS GOFORTH: *What's he wheeling in here that looks like a baby-buggy for a baby from Mars?*

[*He is pushing a 'mock-up' of a portable X-ray machine.*]

BLACKIE: It's something your doctor in Rome, Dr – what? Rengucci? – had sent up here to spare you the trouble of interrupting your work to take a new set of pictures to show what progress there is in the healing of the lesion, the lung-abscess, that –

MRS GOFORTH: Oh, so you're having private consultations with that quack in Rome?

BLACKIE: Just routine calls that he told me to make sure to spare you the trouble of –

MRS GOFORTH: Spare me no trouble, just spare me your goddam PRESUMPTION!

DR LULLO: *Forse più tarde, fors' un po più tarde?*

MRS GOFORTH: *Will you get your sneaky grin out of here? VA. VA. PRESTO!*

[*He retires quickly from the lighted area.* MRS GOFORTH *advances both fearfully and threateningly upon the medical apparatus.*]

My outside is *public*, but my insides are *private*, and the Rome quack was hired by my bitch daughter that wants to hang black crêpe on me. Wants to know if I'm going and when I'll go. Doesn't know that if and when I do go, she gets one dollar, the rest goes to a – a *cultural Foundation!* – named for *me*? Blackie, wheel this thing off the terrace, to the cliffside of the mountain and shove it over!

BLACKIE: Mrs Goforth, you mustn't ask me to do ridiculous things.

MRS GOFORTH: I don't do ridiculous things and don't ask anyone else to do 'em for me. But if you think it's ridiculous of me to show my opinion of Rengucci's presumption and – *Look, watch this! Here we go, perambulator from Mars. Out, down, go!*

[*She thrusts it violently on to the forestage, where it is seized by the* STAGE ASSISTANTS *and rushed into the wings: she crosses on to the forestage, leaning forward to watch its fall off the cliff. After a couple of moments, we hear a muted crash that signifies its destruction on the rocky beach under the mountain. Then she straightens, dizzily, with a fierce laugh, and staggers back toward the library area, where* BLACKIE, *meanwhile, has closed her notebook and rushed off stage.*

Heart-beat sounds as MRS GOFORTH *moves distractedly about the library area, calling out breathlessly for* BLACKIE. *She presses several buttons on the inter-com. box on the desk: electric buzzers sound from here and there on the stage but no one responds: She washes down a pill with a swig of brandy: the heartbeat sounds subside as her agitation passes. She sinks into the desk-chair.*]

MRS GOFORTH: – Ahhh . . .

[*Then she activates her tape-recorder and speaks into it with a voice that is plaintively childlike.*]

– Blackie, the Boss is sorry she took her nerves out on you. It's those night-injections I take nights for my – neuralgia – neuritis – bursitis. The pick-up pills and the quiet-down pills: nerves shot . . .

[*A wave booms under the mountain.*]

– Oh, God, Blackie, I'm *scared*! You know what I'm scared of? Possibly, maybe, the Boss is – *dying* this summer! On the Divina Costiera, under that, that – angry old lion, the sun, and the – insincere sympathy of the – [*Her mood suddenly reverses again.*] No, no, no, I don't want her goddam sympathy, I'll take that slobbery stuff off the tape and – BEGIN! CONTINUE! DICTATION!

[*She rises, paces the forestage with a portable 'mike'.*

    HARMONIUM: *a phrase of lyrical music: she stops short, lifting a jewelled hand as if to say 'Listen' – Then suddenly the hard accretion of years is broken through. The stage dims out except for her follow-spot on the forestage.*]

'Cloudy symbols of a – high romance . . .' – Who said that, where is that from? Check tomorrow, Blackie, in Book of Familiar Quotations . . .

Begin, continue dictation. [*Pause: paces*] – The love of true understanding isn't something a man brings up the road to you every day or once in a blue moon, even. But it was brought to me once, almost too late but not quite . . .

The hard shell of my heart, the calcium deposits grown around it, could still be cracked, broken through, and my last husband broke through it, and I was brought back to life and almost back to – what? – Youth . . .

– The nights, the nights, especially the first one I spent with Alex! – The way that a lover undresses, removes his clothes the first night you pass together, is a clue, a definite clue, to your whole future relationship with him, you know. – Alex unclothed himself *unconsciously gracefully*, as if before no one in a – room made of windows, and then, unclothed – *correction*: clothed in a god's perfection, his naked body! – He went from window to window, all the way round the bedroom, drawing the curtains together so that daybreak beginning wouldn't wake us early from the sleep after love, which is a heavenly sleep that shouldn't be broken early. Then came to rest in a god's perfection beside me: reached up to turn off the light: I reached up and turned it *back on!*

[*At this point,* MRS GOFORTH's *watchdogs (Lupos) set up a great clamour on the inland side of the mountain. A* MAN *shouts.* WOMEN SERVANTS *scream in Italian. Somebody calls, 'Rudy, Rudy!'*

MRS GOFORTH *is very annoyed by this disruption of her tender recollections: she presses various buttons on the inter-com. box on her desk.*]

MRS GOFORTH [*shouting over the dogs*]: CHE SUCCEDE! CHE FA, CRETINI! STRONZE!! (etc.).

[*The savage barking continues but diminishes a little in volume as a* YOUNG MAN, *who has been just assaulted by dogs, limps and stumbles on to the terrace: He bears a heavy white sack over his shoulder: looks back as if to make sure he's no longer pursued.* BLACKIE *appears behind him, panting, looking as if she'd also been roughed-up by the dogs.*]

BLACKIE [*To the* YOUNG MAN]: Places go mad, it's catching, people catch it! [*Draws a breath.*] There's a doctor up here, I'll get him for you.

CHRIS: Can I see Mrs Goforth?

BLACKIE: Sit down somewhere. I'll see if she can see you, and I'll –

[*The young man,* CHRIS, *limps out upon the forestage: sinks on to a white iron bench: a wave crashes below the mountain. He looks blankly out at the audience for a moment: then shakes his head and utters a desperate-sounding laugh.* BLACKIE *rushes into the library area.*]

– Mrs Goforth, I can't stand this sort of thing!

MRS GOFORTH: *What?*

BLACKIE: Those dogs of Rudy's, those wolves, attacked a young man just now.

MRS GOFORTH: What young man, doing what?

BLACKIE: He was climbing the mountain to see you!

MRS GOFORTH: Who is he, what does he want?

BLACKIE: I didn't stop to ask that. I had to drive the dogs off to keep him from being torn to pieces before I – asked him questions: Look! [*She shows* MRS GOFORTH *a laceration on her thigh, just over the knee*] – The others just watched and screamed like children at a circus!

MRS GOFORTH: Sit down, have a brandy. A place like this is always protected by dogs.

[*Sound of another wave crashing.*]

CHRIS: BOOM.

[*He discovers that his leather pants*, lederhosen, *have been split down his thigh.*]

BLACKIE: That gangster's bodyguard, Rudy, just stood there and watched!

MRS GOFORTH: Blackie, this estate contains things appraised by Lloyd's at over two million pounds sterling, besides my jewels and summer furs, and that's why it has to be guarded against trespassers, uninvited intruders. Have you had your anti-tetanus shot, or – whatever they call it?

BLACKIE: Yes, I'm all right but he isn't. [*She presses a button on the intercom. box.*]

MRS GOFORTH: Who're you calling?

BLACKIE: I'm calling Dr Lullo.

MRS GOFORTH: Stop that, leave that to me! Do you think I want to be sued by this trespasser? Get away from my desk. I'm going to buzz Rudy. [*Presses another button.*] Rudy, dov'è Rudy? Io lo voglio in liberia, subito, presto! Capito?

[*The* YOUNG MAN *staggers to his feet and calls:* 'MRS GOFORTH!' MRS GOFORTH *picks up a pair of binoculars and gazes out at the* terrace. BLACKIE *stares at her with consternation.*]

CHRIS: MRS GOFORTH?

[RUDY, *the watchman, in semi-military costume, appears on the* *terrace.*]

RUDY: Shut up, stop that shouting. [*Enters the library area.*]

MRS GOFORTH: Aw. Rudy. What happened, what's the report?

RUDY: I caught this man out there climbing up here from the high-way.

BLACKIE: He set the dogs on him.

MRS GOFORTH: That's what the dogs are here for. Rudy, what's the sign say on the gate on the highway?

RUDY: Private property.

MRS GOFORTH: Just 'Private Property', not 'Beware of Dogs'?

RUDY: There's nothing about dogs down there.

MRS GOFORTH: Well, for Chrissake, put up 'Beware of Dogs', too. Put it up right away. If this man sues me, I've got to prove THERE WAS A BEWARE OF DOGS sign.

BLACKIE: How can you prove what's not true?

MRS GOFORTH [*to* RUDY]: Go on, hurry it up!

[RUDY *exits*. MRS GOFORTH *to* BLACKIE]

Now pull yourself together: what a day! It's too much for me, I'll have to go back to bed . . .

[GIULIO, *the gardener's son, a boy of seventeen, appears on the ter-race.*]

GIULIO [*to the young man, who is applying an antiseptic to his lacera-tions*]: Come va? Meglior?

CHRIS: Sì, meglior, grazie. Do you understand English?

GIULIO: Yes, English.

CHRIS: Good. Would you please tell Mrs Goforth that Mr Christo-pher Flanders is here to see her, and – Oh, give her this book, there's a letter in it, and – ask her if I may see her, don't – don't mention the dogs, just say I – I want very much to see her, if she's willing to see me . . .

[*During this exchange on the forestage,* MRS GOFORTH *has picked up the pair of binoculars.*

GIULIO *knocks at the screen that represents the door between the terrace and the library.*]

MRS GOFORTH: Come in, come in, avante!

[*The boy enters, excitedly.*]

GIULIO: Man bring this up road.

MRS GOFORTH [*Gingerly accepting the book in her hand*]: Young man that dogs bite bring this – [*Squints at book.*] – POEMS! – to me?

GIULIO: This, this, brings! Up mountains!

[*She turns the book and squints at a photograph of the author.*]

MRS GOFORTH: – Man resemble this photo?

[BLACKIE *is still quietly weeping at the desk.*]

GIULIO: Non capito.

MRS GOFORTH: Man! – Uomo! – resemble, look like – this photo!

GIULIO: Yes, this man. This man that dogs bite on mountain.

[*Points out excitedly toward the young man on the bench.*]

MRS GOFORTH: Well, go back out – va fuori e dica – Blackie! Tell him to go back out there and say that I am very upset over the accident with the dogs but that I would like to know why he came here without invitation and that I am not responsible for anybody that comes here without invitation!

BLACKIE [*strongly, rising*]: No, I will not. I will not give a man nearly killed by dogs such an inhuman message.

MRS GOFORTH: He hasn't been seriously hurt, he's standing up now. Listen, he's shouting my name.

[*The* YOUNG MAN *has called '*MRS GOFORTH?*' in a hoarse, panting voice. His shirt and one leg of his* lederhosen *have been nearly stripped off him.*

He has the opposite appearance to that which is ordinarily encountered in poets as they are popularly imagined. His appearance is rough and weathered: his eyes wild, haggard: He has the look of a powerful, battered but still undefeated, fighter.]

CHRIS: *MRS GOFORTH!* [*The call is almost imperious.*]

[*A wave crashes under the mountain:* CHRIS *closes his eyes: opens them: crosses to the lounge chair on the terrace and throws himself down in it, dropping a large canvas sack on the terrace tiles.*

The excited, distant barking of the dogs has now died out.

Female voices are still heard exclaiming at a distance, in Italian.]

MRS GOFORTH [*looking again through her binoculars*]: Pull yourself together. The continent has been over-run by beatniks lately. I've been besieged by them, Blackie. Writers that don't write, painters that don't paint. A bunch of free-loaders, Blackie. They come over here on a Yugoslavian freighter with about a hundred dollars in travellers' cheques and the summer addresses of everybody they think they can free-load on. That's why I'm not so sympathetic about them. Look, I made it, I got it because I made it, but they'll never work for a living as long as there is a name on their sucker-list, Blackie. Now cut the hysterics out, now, and go out there and –

BLACKIE: – *What?*

MRS GOFORTH: Interrogate him for me!

BLACKIE: Interrogate? A badly injured young man?

MRS GOFORTH: *Trespasser!* Get that straight in case he tries to sue me. [*She continues inspecting him through the binoculars.*] Hmm, he's not bad looking in a wild sort of way, but I'm afraid he's a beatnik, he has a beard and looks like he hadn't seen water for bathing purposes in a couple of weeks.

BLACKIE: You would, too, if a pack of wild dogs had attacked you.

MRS GOFORTH: *Watch-dogs, lupos*, defending private property: get that straight. He has on *lederhosen*. Hmm. – The first time I saw Alex, in the Bavarian Alps, he had on *lederhosen* and the right legs for 'em, too. And it's odd, it's a coincidence that I was dictating some recollections of Alex, who was a poet, when this young – *trespasser* – got here. Now if the sweat and – the filthy appearance just come from the dogs' attack on him, I mean from *meeting* the dogs, you can tell by the smell of him while you're talking to him.

BLACKIE: You want me to go out and smell him? I'm not a dog, Mrs Goforth.

MRS GOFORTH: You don't have to be a dog to smell a beatnik. Some-times they smell to high heaven because not washing is almost a religion with 'em, why, last summer one of those ones you see in *Life* and *Look*, came up here. I had to talk to him with a handker-chief held to my nose: it was a short conversation and the last one between us.

[CHRIS *staggers up from the lounge-chair and shouts* 'MRS GOFORTH'.]

MRS GOFORTH: – What impudence, going on shouting at me like that!

BLACKIE: I think the least you could do is go out there yourself and show some decent concern over the dogs' attack on him.

MRS GOFORTH: I'm not going to see him till I've checked with my lawyers about my liability, if any. So be a good scout, a nice Brownie den-mother, and go out there and –

BLACKIE: *Interrogate* him?

MRS GOFORTH: Ask him politely what he wants here, why he came to see me without invitation, and if you get the right answers, put him in the pink villino. And I'll see him later, after my siesta. He might be OK for a while, and I could use some male companionship up here since all I've got is you and Generalissimo Rudy for company this summer. I do need male company, Blackie, that's what I need to be me, the old Sissy Goforth, high, low, jack and the game!

BLACKIE: I'll go see if he's seriously hurt. [*She crosses out, to the terrace, and approaches* CHRIS *limping about the forestage. To* CHRIS.] How are you, are you all right, now?

CHRIS: Not all right: but better. Could I see Mrs Goforth?

BLACKIE: Not yet, not right now, but she told me to put you in the little pink guest house, if you can – walk a little. It's a little way down the mountain.

CHRIS: – Well, thank God, and – [*Tries to lift his sack and stumbles under its weight.*] – Mrs Goforth, of course . . .

BLACKIE [*calling*]: GIULIO! VIENE QUI!

[GIULIO *comes on to the terrace.*]

BLACKIE: – Porta questo sacco al villino rosa.

GIULIO [*lifting sack*]: Pesante! – Dio . . .

BLACKIE: *Tu sei pesante, nella testa!* [*Then to* CHRIS] – You can bathe and rest till Mrs Goforth feels better and is ready to see you.

CHRIS: Oh. – Thanks . . .

[*He follows her off the terrace. The* STAGE ASSISTANTS *fold and remove the screen masking a bed upstage. The bed is small but rococo, and all pink.*

The STAGE ASSISTANTS *return downstage with the screen and wait near* MRS GOFORTH, *who is still watching the terrace scene through her binoculars.*]

MRS GOFORTH [*to herself*]: Ah, God . . . [*Raises a hand unconsciously to a pain in her chest.*]

[*The* STAGE ASSISTANTS *unfold the screen before her, as the library area is dimmed out.*]

Scene Two

The area representing the pink villino is lighted: the light is warm gold afternoon light and striated as if coming through half-open shutters.

A cupid is lowered over the bed by a wire: there are smaller cupids on the four posts of the bed.

BLACKIE, CHRIS, and GIULIO enter the narrow lighted area, the young poet limping. GIULIO bears the canvas sack with difficulty, muttering 'Pesante!'

BLACKIE: Here you are, this is it. Now!

CHRIS: What?

BLACKIE: How are your legs? Mrs Goforth keeps a doctor on the place, a resident physician, and I think he ought to come here and do a proper job on those dog-bites.

CHRIS: They're not that bad, really.

BLACKIE: Have you had shots?

CHRIS: Shots?

BLACKIE: For tetanus?

CHRIS: – Yes, yes, sometime or other. I'm actually just – tired out.

BLACKIE: Giulio, see if the water's running in the bathroom. I'm sure you want to bathe before you rest, Mr Flanders. Oh, oh, no covers on the bed.

CHRIS: Don't bother about covers on it.

BLACKIE: I think, I have an idea, you're going to sleep a good while and you might as well sleep comfortably. Giulio. Covers for bed.

GIULIO: *Dov'è?*

BLACKIE: *Cerca nell' armadio del bagno.*

[GIULIO *exits.* CHRIS *sits down on the foot of the narrow bed: his head falls forward.*]

Mr Flanders!

[*He pulls himself up.*]

Please try to stay awake till the bed's made up and you've bathed.

CHRIS: Your name is –? [*He rises, unsteadily.*]

BLACKIE: Frances Black, called Blackie.

CHRIS: How do you do. Mine's Flanders, Christopher Flanders.

[GIULIO *enters.*]

GIULIO: *Non c'è acqua.*

BLACKIE: Well, tell your papa to turn the water on.

[GIULIO *tosses some pink silk sheets on the bed and runs back out.*]

I hope you don't mind camphor, the smell of camphor.

[*He shakes his head slightly, holding on to a bed post.*]

The water ought to be running in a minute.

CHRIS: I hope there's a shower, a tub wouldn't be safe for me.

I don't think even drowning would wake me up.

BLACKIE: I'll wait here till you've bathed.

CHRIS: It's wonderful here after – yesterday in – Naples . . .

BLACKIE: Would you please get on the other side of the bed and help me spread these sheets?

[*He staggers around the bed: They make it up.*]

CHRIS: You –

BLACKIE: What?

CHRIS: I wondered if you're related to Mrs Goforth or if you're –

BLACKIE: Not related. I'm working for Mrs Goforth: secretarial work: She's writing a sort of – all right, you can sit down, now – she's writing her memoirs and I'm helping her with it, the little, as best I – can . . .

[*He sinks back on to the bed and drops his head in his hands.*]

Mr Flanders, the water's turned on, now.

CHRIS [*staggering up*]: Oh. Good. Thank you. This way?

[*Starts off.*]

BLACKIE: I'll fill the tub for you. Do you want warm or cold water, or –

CHRIS: Cold, please. Let me do it.

BLACKIE: No, just stay on your feet till it's ready for you.

[*She crosses off: sound of running water.*]

[*He sits exhaustedly on the bed: sways: his forehead strikes newel-post which is topped by a cupid: the room is full of painted and carved cupids.*

He looks up at the cupid on the post, shakes his head with a sad, wry grimace and drops his head in his hands and slumps over again.

BLACKIE *returns from the bathroom with a towel-robe. She claps her hands.*]

BLACKIE: I told you to stay on your feet.

CHRIS [*struggling up*]: Sorry. What is – I almost said 'Where am I?'

BLACKIE: Here's a towel-robe for you, you'd better just duck in and out.

[*He crosses to door.*]

CHRIS [*looking back at her from threshold*]: Is this called the Cupid Room?

BLACKIE: I don't know if it's called that but it should be.

[*He starts to enter but remains on threshold.*]

CHRIS: What a remarkable bath-tub, it's almost the size of deck-pool on a steamship.

BLACKIE [*dryly*]: Yes, Mrs Goforth thinks a bath-tub should be built for at least two people.

CHRIS [*entering*]: She must have been to Japan.

BLACKIE: Yes. She probably owns it.

[CHRIS *enters the bathroom: a splash, a loud gasp.*]

BLACKIE: Oh, I should have warned you, it's mountain spring water.

CHRIS: Does it come from a glacier?

[BLACKIE *picks up the cords of his rucksack to drag it away from the bedside. She finds it startlingly heavy.*

She kneels beside it to loosen the draw-strings, draws out a silvery section of some metal-work.

Rises guiltily as CHRIS *reappears in the towel-robe.*]

BLACKIE: You're – shivering.

CHRIS: For exercise; shivering's good exercise.

BLACKIE: I don't think you need any more exercise for a while. – How did you get this sack of yours up the mountain?

CHRIS: Carried it – from Genoa.

BLACKIE: I could hardly drag it away from the bed.

CHRIS: Yes, it's heavy with metal, I work in metal, now, I construct mobiles, but it's not the mobiles that are heavy, it's the metalsmith tools.

BLACKIE: You, uh – sell – mobiles, do you?

CHRIS: No, mostly give 'em away. Of course I –

BLACKIE: – What?

CHRIS: Some things aren't made to be sold, oh, you sell them, but they're not made for that, not for selling, they're made for –

BLACKIE: Making them?

CHRIS: Is there something buzzing in the room or is the buzz in my head? Oh, a wasp, it'll fly back out the shutters, is this a cigarette box? [*Opens box on small bedside table.*] Empty.

BLACKIE: – Have a Nazionale. [*Offers him the pack.*]

CHRIS: Thank you.

BLACKIE: I'll leave the pack here, I have more in my room. – Your hair's not dry, it's still wet.

[*He shakes his head like a spaniel.*]

Dry it with the towel and get right into bed, I have to get back to work now. I work here, I do secretarial work and I –

CHRIS: Don't go right away.

BLACKIE: You need to rest, right away.

CHRIS: The ice water woke me up.

BLACKIE: Just temporarily, maybe.

CHRIS: I'll rest much better if I know a bit more, such as – Did Mrs Goforth remember who I was?

BLACKIE: I don't know about that but she liked your looks, if that's any comfort to you.

CHRIS: I didn't see her. She saw me?

BLACKIE: She inspected you through a pair of military fieldglasses before she had me take you to the pink villa with the – king-size bath-tub, the pink silk sheets and the cupids.

CHRIS: Do they, uh – signify something?

BLACKIE: Everything signifies something. I'll – I'll shut the shutters and you get into bed. [*Turns away from him.*]

CHRIS [*sitting on the bed*]: What is the programme for me when I wake up?

BLACKIE [*her back still toward him*]: Don't you make out your own programmes?

CHRIS: Not when I'm visiting people. I try to adapt myself as well as I can to their programmes, when I'm – visiting people.

BLACKIE: Is that much of the time?

CHRIS: Yes, that's – *most* of the time . . .

BLACKIE: Well, I think you're in for a while, if you play your cards right. You do want to be in, don't you? After hauling that sack all the way from Genoa and up this mountain to Mrs Goforth? Or have the pink silk sheets and the cupids scared you, worse than the dogs you ran into?

CHRIS: You have a sharp tongue, Blackie.

BLACKIE: I'm sorry but I was mistaken when I thought I had strong nerves. They're finished for today if not for the season, for – years . . . [*She starts away.*]

CHRIS: Have a cigarette with me. [*He extends the pack to her.*]

BLACKIE: You want to get some more information from me?

CHRIS: I'd sleep better if I knew a bit more.

BLACKIE: I wouldn't be too sure of *that*.

CHRIS: I've heard, I've been told, that Mrs Goforth hasn't been well lately.

[BLACKIE *laughs as if startled.*]

CHRIS: She's lucky to have you with her.

BLACKIE: – Why?

CHRIS: I can see you're – sympathetic and understanding about Mrs Goforth's – condition, but – not sentimental about it. – Aren't I right about that?

BLACKIE: I'm not understanding about it and I'm afraid I've stopped being sympathetic. Mrs Goforth is a dying monster. [*Rises.*] *Sorry: I'm talking too much!*

CHRIS: No, not enough. Go on.

BLACKIE: Why do you want to hear it?

CHRIS: I've climbed a mountain and fought off a wolf-pack to see her.

BLACKIE: – *Why?*

CHRIS: Nowhere else to go, now.

BLACKIE: Well, that's an honest admission.

CHRIS: Let's stick to honest admissions.

BLACKIE [*sitting back down by the bed*]: All right. I'll give you something to sleep on. You'll probably wish I hadn't but here it is. She eats nothing but pills: around the clock. And at night she has nightmares in spite of morphine injections. I rarely sleep a night through without an electric buzzer by my bed waking me up. I tried ignoring the buzzer, but found out that if I did she'd come stumbling out of her bedroom, on to the terrace, raving into a microphone that's connected to a tape-recorder, stumbling about and raving her –

CHRIS: Raving?

BLACKIE: Yes, her demented memoirs, her memories of her career as a great international beauty which she thinks she still is. I'm here, employed here, to – take down and type up these –

CHRIS: Memories?

BLACKIE: – That's enough for you now. Don't you think so?

CHRIS: She doesn't know she's –?

BLACKIE: Dying? Oh no! Won't face it! Apparently never thought that her – legendary – existence – could go on less than forever! Insists she's only suffering from neuralgia, neuritis, allergies and bursitis! Well? Can you still sleep? After this – bed-time story?

CHRIS: – Blackie, I've had a good bit of experience with old dying ladies, scared to death of dying, ladies with lives like Mrs Goforth's behind them, which they won't think are over, and I've discovered it's possible to give them, at least to offer them, something closer to what they need than what they think they still want. Yes . . . Would you please throw me the strings of my sack, Blackie?

[*She tosses the strings to the bedside: He hauls the rucksack over, leans out of the bed to open it: removes a mobile.*]

– Give her this for me, Blackie. It took me six months to make it. It has a name, a title, it's called 'The Earth Is a Wheel in a Great Big Gambling Casino'.

[*The* HARMONIUM PLAYER, *in his dim upstage light, starts playing softly.*]

BLACKIE: – 'The Earth Is –'?

CHRIS: 'A Wheel in a Great Big Gambling Casino'. I made it on hinges, it has to be unfolded before it's hung up. I think you'd better hang it up before you show it to her, if you don't mind, and in a place where it will turn in the wind, so it will make a – more impressive – impression . . .

– And this is for you, this book? [*He hands a book to her.*]

BLACKIE: Poems?

CHRIS: It's a verse-adaptation I made of the writings of a Swami, a great Hindu teacher, my – teacher. Oh. One thing more. I'd like to make a phone-call to a friend, an invalid lady, in Sicily – Taormina, a mountain above Taormina. – Would Mrs Goforth object if I –?

BLACKIE: Not if she doesn't know. What's the number?

[*He gives her the number. She makes the call in Italian and is told that it will not go through for some time.*]

– There'll be a delay: is it very important?

CHRIS: Yes, it is: she's dying. – Blackie? You're the kindest person I've met in a long, long time . . .

BLACKIE [*drawing a sheet over him*]: This sort of thing is just automatic in women.

CHRIS: Only in some of them, Blackie. [*His eyes fall shut.*]

BLACKIE: You're falling asleep.

CHRIS: – Yes, automatic – like kindness in some women . . .

[*He drops his cigarette and she picks it up and crosses to the phone.*]

BLACKIE: [*into phone*]: Mariella? Bring a tray of food up to the pink villa: Better make it cold things: the guest's asleep and won't wake up for hours. [*She hangs up, looks at* CHRIS *and exits with book.*]

[*Light dims on this area and a spot of light immediately hits* MRS GOFORTH *on terrace.*

The STAGE ASSISTANTS *have set a screen before the area and light is brought up on the forestage which represents the terrace of the white villa. The* STAGE ASSISTANTS *remove a wide screen and we see* MRS GOFORTH *with two servants,* GIULIO *and* SIMONETTA. MRS GOFORTH *is preparing to take a sun-bath on the terrace. Her appearance is bizarre. She has on a silk robe covered with the signs of the zodiac, and harlequin sunglasses with purple lenses.*]

MRS GOFORTH [*in her very 'pidgin' Italian*]: Table here. Capite? Tabolo. [*Points.*] Qui. On tabolo, I want – What are you grinning at?

GIULIO [*very Neapolitan*]: Niente, niente, mascusa! [*Places table by chaise.*]

SIMONETTA [*giggling*]: Tabolo.

MRS GOFORTH: On tabolo voglio – una bottoglia d'acqua minerable, San Pellegrino, capite, molto ghiaccato: capite?

[SIMONETTA *giggles behind her hand at* GIULIO's *antic deference to the Signora.*

MRS GOFORTH *glares suspiciously from one to the other, turning from side to side like a bull wondering which way to charge.*

BLACKIE *enters the terrace area with the mobile, folded.*]

MRS GOFORTH: *Che stronze!* Both of 'em.

BLACKIE: You mustn't call them that, it has an insulting meaning.

MRS GOFORTH: I know what it means and that's what I mean it to mean. Generalissimo Rudy says they sleep together and carry on together some nights right here on my terrace.

BLACKIE: They're from Naples, and –

MRS GOFORTH: What's that got to do with it?

BLACKIE: – And Generalissimo Rudy wants the girl for himself, so he –

MRS GOFORTH: WILL YOU PLEASE TELL THEM WHAT I WANT ON THE TABLE BY THIS CHAISE. HERE?

BLACKIE: What do you want on the table?

MRS GOFORTH: I – want a cold bottle of acqua minerale, cigarettes, matches, my Bain-Soleil, my codeine and empirin tablets, a shot of cognac on the rocks, the *Paris Herald-Tribune*, *The Rome Daily American*, *The Wall Street Journal*, *The London Times* and *Express*, the – – Hey, what did you do with the –

BLACKIE: The visitor?

MRS GOFORTH: The beatnik trespasser, yes, and what the hell have you got there that rattles like a string of box cars crossing a railyard switch?

BLACKIE: The young man's in the pink villa where you told me to put him – this is something he gave me for me to give you. It seems he constructs mobiles.

MRS GOFORTH: Mobiles? Constructs?

BLACKIE: Yes, those metal decorations. He gives them titles: this one's called 'The Earth is a Wheel in a Great Big Gambling Casino'.

MRS GOFORTH: Is it a present or something he hopes he can sell me?

BLACKIE: It's a present. He wanted me to suspend it before you saw it, but since you've already seen it – shall I hang it up somewhere?

MRS GOFORTH: No, just put it down somewhere and help me up, the sun is making me dizzy, I don't know why I came out here. What am I doing out here?

BLACKIE: I was going to remind you that Dr Rengucci warned you not to expose yourself to the sun till the chest abscess, the lesion, has healed completely.

MRS GOFORTH: I DON'T HAVE A CHEST ABSCESS! – stop putting bad mouth on me! Open the door, I'm going in the library.

[*The* STAGE ASSISTANTS *rush out and remove the screen masking that area as* MRS GOFORTH *starts toward it, lifting a hand like a Roman empress saluting the populace.*
She enters the library area.]

What did he have to say?

BLACKIE: The –?

MRS GOFORTH: *Trespasser*, what did he have to say?

BLACKIE: About what?

MRS GOFORTH: *ME.*

BLACKIE: He wondered if you remembered him or not.

MRS GOFORTH: Oh, I might have met him somewhere, sometime or other, when I was still meeting people, interested in it, before they all seemed like the same person over and over and I got tired of the person.

BLACKIE: This young man won't seem like the same person to you.

MRS GOFORTH: That remains to be – Blackie, y'know what I need to shake off this, this – depression, what would do me more good this summer than all the shots and pills in the pharmaceutical kingdom? I need me a lover.

BLACKIE: What do you mean by 'a lover'?

MRS GOFORTH: I mean a lover! What do *you* mean by a lover, or is that word outside your Vassar vocabulary?

BLACKIE: I've only had one lover, my husband Charles, and I lost Charles last spring.

MRS GOFORTH: What beats me is how you could have a husband named Charles and not call him Charlie. I mean the fact that you called him Charles and not Charlie describes your whole relationship with him, don't it?

BLACKIE [*flaring*]: *Stop about my husband!*

MRS GOFORTH: The dead are dead and the living are living!

BLACKIE: Not so, I'm not dead but not living!

MRS GOFORTH: GIULIO!

[*He has entered the library area with the mineral water.*]

MRS GOFORTH: Va a villino rosa e portame qui the sack – il sacco, SACCO! – delle hospite la.

BLACKIE: Oh, no, you mustn't do that, that's too undignified of you!

[GIULIO *exits to perform this errand.*]

MRS GOFORTH: Take care of your own dignity and lemme take care of mine. It's a perfectly natural, legitimate thing to do, to go through the luggage of a trespasser on your place for – possible – weapons, and so forth . . . [*Sits at desk.*] Pencil, notebook, dictation.

[BLACKIE *pays no attention to these demands: lights a cigarette behind* MRS GOFORTH'*s back as she begins dictating.*]

– Season of '24, costume ball at Cannes. Never mind the style, now, polish up later . . .

– Went as Lady Godiva. All of me, gilded, my whole body painted gold, except for – green velvet fig leaves. Breasts? Famous breasts? Nude, nude completely!

– Astride a white horse, led into the ballroom by a young nigger. Correction. A Nubian – slave-boy. Appearance created a riot. Men clutched at my legs, trying to dismount me so they could *mount* me. Maddest party ever, ever imaginable in those days of mad parties. This set the record for madness. – In '29, so much ended, but not for me. I smelt the crash coming, animal instinct – very valuable asset, put everything into absolutely indestructible utilities such as – chemicals, *electric* . . . minerals.

[GIULIO *enters with the rucksack.*]

GIULIO: Ecco, il sacco! [*Drops it before* MRS GOFORTH *with a crash that makes her gasp.*]

BLACKIE: May I be excused? I don't want to take part in this.

MRS GOFORTH: Stay here. You heard that noise, that wasn't just clothes, that was metal.

BLACKIE: Yes, I suppose he's come here to seize the mountain by force of arms.

MRS GOFORTH [*to* GIULIO]: Giulio, open, *apierte!*

[GIULIO *opens the sack and the inspection begins.*]

BLACKIE: I told you he made mobiles, the sack's full of metalsmith's tools.

MRS GOFORTH: He hauled this stuff up the mountain?

BLACKIE: It didn't fly up.

MRS GOFORTH: He must have the back of a dray horse. Tell this idiot to hold the sack upside down and empty it all on the floor, he's taking things out like it was a Christmas stocking.

BLACKIE: I'll do it. He'd break everything. [*She carefully empties the contents of the sack on to the floor*].

MRS GOFORTH: See if he's got any travellers' cheques and how much they amount to.

BLACKIE [*ignoring this order and picking up a book*]: He offered me this book, I forgot to take it.

MRS GOFORTH [*glaring at the book through her glasses*]: 'Meanings Known and Unknown'. It sounds like something religious.

BLACKIE: He says it's a verse-adaptation he did of a –

MRS GOFORTH: Swami Something. See if you can locate the little book they always carry with names and addresses in it, sometimes it gives you a clue to their backgrounds and – inclinations. Here. This is it. [*Snatches up an address book.*] – Christ. Lady Emerald Fowler, she's been in hell for ten years. – Christabel Smithers, that name rings a long ago church bell for a dead bitch, too. Mary Cole, *dead!* Laurie Emerson, *dead!* Is he a graveyard sexton? My God, where's his passport?

BLACKIE [*picking it up*]: Here.

MRS GOFORTH: Date of birth, 1928: hmmm, no chicken, Blackie. How old's that make him?

BLACKIE: – Thirty-four. [*Lights a cigarette.* MRS GOFORTH *coughs and snatches the cigarette from* BLACKIE's *hand. She sets it on the desk and in a moment will start smoking it herself.*]

MRS GOFORTH: No travellers' cheques whatsoever. Did he have some cash on him?

BLACKIE: I don't know, I neglected to frisk him.

MRS GOFORTH: Did you get him to bathe?

BLACKIE: Yes.

MRS GOFORTH: How'd he look in the bath-tub?

BLACKIE: I'm afraid I can't give you any report on that.

MRS GOFORTH: Where's his clothes, no clothes, *niente vestiti in sacco?*

[GIULIO *produces one shirt, laundered but not ironed.*]

GIULIO: *Ecco, una cammicia, una bella cammicia!*

MRS GOFORTH: One shirt!

BLACKIE: He probably had to check some of his luggage somewhere, in order to get up the – goat path . . . and the clothes he had on were demolished by Rudy's dogs.

MRS GOFORTH: Well, put a robe in his room: I know: the Samurai warrior's robe that Alex wore at breakfast, we always wore robes at breakfast in case he wanted to go back to bed right after . . .

[STAGE ASSISTANT *enters with robe: sword belt attached.*]

BLACKIE: Did he keep the sword on him at breakfast?

MRS GOFORTH: Yes, he did and sometimes he'd draw it out of the scabbard and poke me with it. Ho, ho. Tickle me with the point of it, ho ho ho ho!

BLACKIE: You weren't afraid he'd – accidentally –?

MRS GOFORTH: Sure, and it was exciting. I had me a little revolver. I'd draw a bead on him sometimes and I'd say, you are too beautiful to live and so you have to die, now, tonight – tomorrow –

[STAGE ASSISTANT *has handed the robe to* BLACKIE *who accepts it without a glance at him.*]

– put the robe in the pink villino, and then call the Witch of Capri.

BLACKIE: Which witch?

MRS GOFORTH: The one that wired me last month. 'Are you still living?' Tell her I am. And get her over for dinner, tell her it's *urgentissimo!* Everything's *urgentissimo* here this summer . . .

[*Phone buzzes on desk. As* BLACKIE *starts off,* MRS GOFORTH *answers the phone.*]

Pronto, pronto, chi parla? – Taormina? Sicilia? – I've placed no call to that place. [*Slams phone.*] – Hmmmm, the summer is coming to life! I'm coming back to life with it! [*She presses buttons on her intercom. system: electric buzzers sound from various points on the stage as the* STAGE ASSISTANTS *cover the library area with the griffin-crested screen.*]

DIM OUT

Scene Three

That evening: the terrace of the white villa and a small section of MRS GOFORTH's bedroom, upstage left.

In this scene, the STAGE ASSISTANTS may double as butlers, with or without white jackets.

At rise: two screens are lighted, one masking the small dinner table on the forestage, the other MRS GOFORTH. A STAGE ASSISTANT stands beside each screen so that they can be removed simultaneously when a chord on the harmonium provides the signal.

The middle panel of MRS GOFORTH's screen is topped by a gold-winged griffin to signify that she is 'in residence' behind it.

MRS GOFORTH'S VOICE [asthmatically]: Simonetta, la roba.

[SIMONETTA rushes behind the screen with an elaborate Oriental costume.]

Attenzione, goddam it, questa roba molto, molto valore. Va bene. Adesso, perruga!*
SIMONETTA [Emerging from the screen]: La perrucha bionde?
MRS GOFORTH: Nero, nero!

[The MUSICIAN strikes a ready chord on the harmonium: the screens are whisked away. In the stage left area, we see MRS GOFORTH in the Oriental robe, on the forestage, RUDY in his semi-military outfit pouring himself a drink, and a small section of balustrade on which is a copper brazier, flickering with blue flame. BLACKIE enters, stage

* Wig.

right, with a napkin and silver and sets a third place at the table. RUDY *hovers behind her.*]

BLACKIE: Stop breathing down my neck.

MRS GOFORTH: Ecco!

[*She puts on a black Kabuki wig with fantastic ornaments stuck in it. Her appearance is gorgeously bizarre.*

As she moves, now, out upon the forestage, the harmonium, outlined dimly against a starry night sky, plays a bit of Oriental music.]

Well, no comment, Blackie.

BLACKIE: The Witch of Capri has just gotten out of the boat and is getting into the funicular.

MRS GOFORTH: You kill me, Blackie, you do, you literally kill me. I come out here in this fantastic costume and all you say is the Witch of Capri has landed.

BLACKIE: I told you how fantastic it was when you wore it last weekend when that Italian screen star didn't show up for dinner, so I didn't think it would be necessary to tell you again, but what I do want to tell you is that I wish you'd explain to Rudy that I find him resistible, and when I say resistible I'm putting it as politely as I know how.

MRS GOFORTH: What's Rudy doing to you?

BLACKIE: Standing behind me, and –

MRS GOFORTH: You want him in front of you, Blackie.

BLACKIE: I want him off the terrace while I'm on it.

MRS GOFORTH: Rudy, you'd better go check my bedroom safe. These rocks I've put on tonight are so hot they're radioactive. [*To* BLACKIE.] Guess what I'm worth on the hoof in this regalia.

BLACKIE: I'm no good at guessing the value of –

MRS GOFORTH: I can't stand anything false. Even my kidney-stones, if I had kidney-stones, would be genuine diamonds fit for a queen's crown, Blackie.

[BLACKIE *lights a cigarette.* MRS GOFORTH *takes the cigarette from her.*]

A witch and a bitch always dress up for each other, because otherwise the witch would upstage the bitch, or the bitch would upstage the witch, and the result would be havoc.

BLACKIE: Fine feathers flying in all directions?

MRS GOFORTH: That's right. – The Witch has a fairly large collection of rocks herself, but no important pieces. [*Crosses, smoking, to the table.*] Hey. The table's set for three. Are you having dinner with us?

BLACKIE: Not this evening, thanks, I have to catch up on my typing.

MRS GOFORTH: Then who's this third place set for?

BLACKIE: The young man in the pink villa, I thought he'd be dining with you.

MRS GOFORTH: That was presumptuous of you. He's having no meals with me till I know more about him. The Witch of Capri can give me the low-down on him: in fact, the only reason I asked the Witch to dinner was to get the low-down on this mountain climber.

THE WITCH [*at a distance*]: Yoo-hoo!

MRS GOFORTH: YOOO-HOOO! She won't be here more than a minute before she makes some disparaging comment on my appearance. Codeine, empirin, brandy, before she gets here; she takes a morbid interest in the health of her friends because her own's on the down-grade.

THE WITCH [*nearer*]: Yoo-hoo!

MRS GOFORTH: Yooo-hooo! Here she comes, here comes the Witch.

[THE WITCH *of Capri, the Marchesa Constance Ridgeway-Condotti, appears on the terrace. She looks like a creature out of a sophisticated fairy tale, her costume like something that might have been designed for Fata Morgana. Her dress is grey chiffon, panelled, and on her blue-tinted head she wears a cone-shaped hat studded with pearls, the peak of it draped with the material of her dress, her expressive, claw-like hands a-glitter with gems. At the sight of* MRS GOFORTH, *she halts dramatically, opening her eyes very wide for a moment, as if confronted by a frightening apparition: then she utters a dramatic little cry and extends her arms in a counterfeit gesture of pity.*]

THE WITCH: *Sissy! Love!*

MRS GOFORTH: Connie . . .

[*They embrace ritually and coolly: then stand back from each other with sizing-up stares.*]

THE WITCH: Sissy, don't tell me we're having a Chinese dinner.

MRS GOFORTH: This isn't a Chinese robe, it's a Kabuki dancer's, a Japanese national treasure that Simon Willingham bought me on our reconciliation trip to Japan. It's only some centuries old. I had to sneak it through customs – Japanese customs – by wearing it tucked up under a chinchilla coat. Y'know I studied Kabuki, and got to be very good at it, I was a guest artist once at a thing for typhoon relief, and I can still do it, you see.

[*She opens her lacquered fan and executes some Kabuki dance steps, humming weirdly: the effect has a sort of grotesque beauty, but she is suddenly dizzy and staggers against the table.* THE WITCH *utters a shrill cry:* BLACKIE *rushes to catch her and the table.* MRS GOFORTH *tries to laugh it off.*]

MRS GOFORTH: – Ha, ha, too much codeine, I took a little codeine for my neuralgia before you got here.

THE WITCH: Well, I'm suffering, too. We're suffering together. Will you look at my arm. [*Draws up her flowing sleeves to expose a bandaged forearm.*] The sea is full of Medusas.

MRS GOFORTH: Full of what?

THE WITCH: Medusas, you know, those jelly-fish that sting, the Latins call them Medusas, and one of them got me this morning, a giant one, at the Piccola Marina. I want a martini. I've got to stay slightly drunk to bear the pain. [*She tosses her parasol to* BLACKIE *and advances to the liquor cart.*] Sissy, your view is a *meraviglia, veramente una meraviglia!* [*Drains a martini that* BLACKIE *pours her: then swings full circle and dizzily returns to a chair at the table.*] Do we have to eat? – I'm so full of canapés from Mona's cocktail do . . .

MRS GOFORTH: Oh, is that what you're full of? We're having a very light supper, because the smell of food after codeine nauseates me, Connie.

BLACKIE: Mrs Goforth, shouldn't I take something to your house-guest since he's not dining with you?

MRS GOFORTH: No, meaning no, but you can leave us now, Blackie. Oh, excuse me, this is my secretary, Miss Black. Blackie, this is – what's your latest name, Connie?

THE WITCH: I mailed you my wedding invitation the spring before last spring to some hospital in Boston, the Leahey Clinic, and never received a word of acknowledgement from you.

MRS GOFORTH: Oh, weddings and funerals're things you show up at or you don't, according to where you are and – [*Rings bell for service:* the STAGE ASSISTANTS *appear with white towels over their forearms or coloured mess-jackets.* NOTE: *Although they sometimes take part in the action of the play, the characters in the play never appear to notice the* STAGE ASSISTANTS.] – *other* circumstances: Have a gull's egg, Connie.

THE WITCH: No, thank you, I can't stand gulls.

MRS GOFORTH: Well, eating their eggs cuts down on their population.

THE WITCH: What is this monster of the deep?

MRS GOFORTH: Dentice, dentice freddo.

THE WITCH: It has a horried expression on its face.

MRS GOFORTH: Don't look at it, just eat it.

THE WITCH: Couldn't possibly, thank you.

MRS GOFORTH: – Are you still living on blood transfusions, Connie? That's not good, it turns you into a vampire, a pipistrella, ha ha . . . Your neck's getting too thin, Connie. Is it true you had that sheep embryo – plantation in – Switzerland? I heard so: don't approve of it. It keys you up for a while and then you collapse, completely. The human system can't stand too much stimulation after – sixty . . .

THE WITCH: What did they find out at the Leahey Clinic, Sissy?

MRS GOFORTH: Oh, *that*, that was just a little – routine check-up . . .

THE WITCH: When you called me today I was so relieved I could die: shouted 'Hallelujah' silently, to myself. I'd heard such distressing rumours about you lately, Sissy.

MRS GOFORTH: Rumours? Hell, what rumours?

THE WITCH [*crossing to bar cart for a refill*]: I can't tell you the rumours that have been circulating about you since your house-party last month. The ones you brought over from Capri came back to Capri with stories that I love you too much to repeat.

MRS GOFORTH: Repeat them, Connie, repeat them.

THE WITCH: Are you sure you feel well enough to take them? [*Returns to her chair.*] Well – they said you were, well, that you seemed to be off your rocker. They said you spent the whole night shouting over loudspeakers so nobody could sleep and that what you shouted was not to be *believed*!

MRS GOFORTH: Oh, how *nice* of them, Connie, Capri's turned into a nest of vipers, Connie – and the sea is full of Medusas? Mmm. The Medusas are spawned by the bitches. You want to know the truth behind this gossip? Or would you rather believe a pack of malicious inventions?

THE WITCH: You know I love you, Sissy. What's the truth?

MRS GOFORTH: Not *that*. – I'll tell you the truth. [*Rises and indicates the inter-com. speaker.*] I'm writing my memoirs, this summer. I've got the whole place wired for sound, a sort of very elaborate inter-com. or walkie-talkie system, so I can dictate to my secretary, Blackie. I buzz my secretary any time of the day and night and continue dictating to her. That's the truth, the true story. [*Crosses to* THE WITCH.]

THE WITCH [*holding her hand*]: I'm so glad you told me, Sissy, love!

MRS GOFORTH: Has it ever struck you, Connie, that life is all memory except for the one present moment that goes by you so quick you hardly catch it going? It's really all memory, Connie, except for each passing moment. What I just now said to you is a memory now – recollection. Uh-hummm . . . [*She paces the terrace.*] – I'm up now. When I was at the table is a memory, now. [*Arrives at edge of lighted area Down Right and turns.*] – When I turned at the other end of the terrace is a memory now . . .

[THE WITCH *crosses to her.*]

Practically everything is a memory to me, now, so I'm writing my memoirs . . . [*Points up.*] Shooting star: it's shot: – a memory now. Six husbands, all memory now. All lovers: all memory now.

THE WITCH: So you're writing your memoirs.

MRS GOFORTH: Devoting all of me to it and all of my time . . . At noon today, I was dictating to Blackie on a tape-recorder: the beautiful part of my life, my love with Alex, my final marriage: Alex.

THE WITCH [*crossing to bar cart*]: Oh, the young Russian dancer from the Diaghilev troupe?

MRS GOFORTH [*crossing back to her chair*]: Oh, God, no, I never married a dancer. Slept with a couple but never married a one. They're too narcissus for me, love only mirrors. Nope. Alex was a young poet with a spirit that was as beautiful as his body. Only one I married that wasn't rich as Croesus. Alex made love without mirrors. He used my eyes for his mirrors. The only husband I've had of the six I've had that I could make love to with a bright light burning over the bed. Hundred watt bulbs overhead! To see, while we loved . . .

THE WITCH [*also back at the table, with the pitcher of martinis*]: – Are you dictating this? Over a loudspeaker?

MRS GOFORTH: – Ah, God – Alex . . .

THE WITCH: – Are you in pain? Do you have a pain in your chest?

MRS GOFORTH: – Why?

THE WITCH: You keep touching your chest.

MRS GOFORTH: – Emotion, I've been very emotional all day . . . At noon today, a young poet came up the goat-path from the highway just as I was in the emotional – throes – of dictating my memories of young Alex . . .

THE WITCH: Ah-ha. [*Finishes her martini.*]

MRS GOFORTH: He came up the goat-path from the Amalfi Drive wearing lederhosen like Alex was wearing the first time I set eyes on Alex.

THE WITCH [*starts to pour another martini*]: Ahh-ha!

MRS GOFORTH [*snatching the pitcher from her and placing it on the floor*]: – Do you want to hear this story?

THE WITCH: Liquor improves my concentration. Go on. You've met a new poet. What was the name of this poet?

MRS GOFORTH: His name was on the book.

THE WITCH: Yes, sometimes they do put the author's name on a book.

The Milk Train Doesn't Stop Here Anymore

MRS GOFORTH [*unamused*]: Sanders? No. Manders? No.

THE WITCH: Flanders. Christopher Flanders. [*Makes large eyes.*] Is he still in circulation?

MRS GOFORTH: I don't know if he's in circulation or not but I do know he came up here to see me and not by the boat and funicular he –

THE WITCH [*crossing to her*]: Well, God help you, Sissy.

MRS GOFORTH: Why, is something wrong with him?

THE WITCH: Not if you're not superstitious. Are you superstitious?

MRS GOFORTH: What's superstition got to do with –

THE WITCH: I've got to have a wee drop of brandy on this!

[*Crosses to bar cart.*] This is really uncanny!

MRS GOFORTH: *Well, come out with it, what?*

THE WITCH [*selecting the brandy bottle*]: I think I'd rather not tell you.

MRS GOFORTH [*commandingly*]: *WHAT?*

THE WITCH: Promise me not to be frightened?

MRS GOFORTH: When've I ever been frightened? Of what? Not even that stiletto you've got for a tongue can scare me!

[*Downs her own martini at a gulp.*] So what's the –?

THE WITCH: Chris, poor Chris Flanders, he has the bad habit of coming to call on a lady just a step or two ahead of the undertaker. [*She sits.*] Last summer at Portofino he stayed with some Texas oil people and at supper one night that wicked old Duke of Parma, you know the one that we call the Parma Violet, he emptied a champagne bottle on Christopher's head and he said, I christen thee, Christopher Flanders, the 'Angel of Death'. The name has stuck to him, Sissy. Why, some people in our age bracket, we're senior citizens, Sissy, would set their dogs on him if he entered their grounds, but since you're not superstitious. – Why isn't he dining here with us?

MRS GOFORTH: I wanted some information about him before I –

THE WITCH: Let him stay here?

MRS GOFORTH: He's here on probation. [*She rings for* GIULIO *and crosses centre.*] I put him in the pink villa where he's been sleeping since noon, when he climbed up a goat-path to see me.

THE WITCH [*following*]: I hope he's not playing his sleeping trick on you, Sissy.

MRS GOFORTH: Trick? Sleeping?

THE WITCH: Yes, last summer when he was with that Portofino couple from Texas, they were thrown into panic when they heard his nickname, Angel of Death, and told him that night to check out in the morning. Well, that night, he swallowed some sleeping pills that night, Sissy, but of course he took the precaution of leaving an early morning call so he could be found and revived before the pills could –

[MRS GOFORTH *abruptly leaves.*]

– Where're you going, Sissy?

MRS GOFORTH: Follow me to the pink villa, hurry, hurry, I better make sure he's not playing that trick on me.

[*She rushes off stage.* THE WITCH *laughs wickedly as she follows. The* STAGE ASSISTANTS *immediately set a screen before this acting area and it dims: then they remove a screen upstage and we see* CHRIS *asleep in the pink villa.*

HARMONIUM: *Variation of a lullaby, perhaps Brahms!*

MRS GOFORTH *and* THE WITCH *appear just on the edge of the small lighted area.*]

MRS GOFORTH: Everything's pink in this villa so it's called the pink villa.

THE WITCH: I see, that's logical, Sissy. Hmmm. There he is: sleeping.

MRS GOFORTH [*in a shrill whisper as they draw closer to the bed*]: Can you tell if he's –?

[THE WITCH *removes her slippers, creeps to the bedside and touches his wrist.*]

– Well?

THE WITCH: Hush! [*Slips back to* MRS GOFORTH.] You're lucky, Sissy. His pulse seems normal, he's sleeping normally, and he has a good colour. – Let me see if there's liquor on his breath. [*Slips back to bed and bends her face to his.*] No. It's sweet as a baby's.

MRS GOFORTH: Don't go to bed with him!

THE WITCH: No, that's your privilege, Sissy.

MRS GOFORTH [*moving downstage from the lighted area in a follow spot*]: Come out here.

THE WITCH [*reluctantly following*]: You must have met him before.

MRS GOFORTH: Oh, somewhere, sometime, when I was still meeting people, before they all seemed like the same person over and over and I got tired of the – person.

THE WITCH: You know his story, don't you?

[*The* STAGE ASSISTANTS *place a section of balustrade, at an angle, beside them, and the copper brazier with the blue flame in it. The flame flickers eerily on* THE WITCH*'s face as she tells what she knows of* CHRIS: *Harmonium plays under the stylized recitation.*]

Sally Ferguson found him at a ski lodge in Nevada where he was working as a ski instructor.

MRS GOFORTH: A poet, a ski instructor?

THE WITCH: Everything about him was like that, a contradiction. He taught Sally skiing at this Nevada lodge where Sally was trying to prove she was a generation younger than she was and thought she could get away with it. – Well, she should have stuck to the gentle slopes, since her bones had gone dry, but one day she took the ski lift to the top of the mountain, drank a hot buttered rum, and took off like a wild thing, a crazy bird, down the mountain, slammed into a tree and broke her hip bone. Well, Christopher Flanders carried her back to the ski lodge. We all thought she was done for but Chris worked a miracle on her that lasted for quite a while. He got her back on her pins after they'd pinned her broken hip together with steel pins. They travelled together, to and from Europe together, but then one time in rough weather, on the promenade deck of one of the Queen ships, the *Mary*, he suddenly let go of her, she took a spill and her old hip bone broke again, too badly for steel pins to pin her back together again, and Sally gave up her travels except from one room to another, on a rolling couch pushed by Chris. We all advised her to let Chris go like Chris had let go of her on the promenade deck of the *Mary*. Would she? Never! She called him my saint, my angel, till the day that she died. And her children contested her will so that Chris got nothing, just his poems published, dedicated to Sally. The book won a prize of some kind and *Vogue* and *Harper's Bazaar* played it up big with lovely photos of Chris looking like what she called him, an angel, a saint . . .

MRS GOFORTH: Did he sleep with that old Ferguson bitch? Or was he just her Death Angel?

> [*Phone rings on the bedside table: the area has remained softly lighted.* CHRIS *starts up: drops back, feigning sleep, as* MRS GOFORTH *rushes to the phone, snatches it up.*]

– Pronto, dica. – Taormina, Sicily? No, Spogliato!

> [*Looks with angry suspicion at* CHRIS, *who murmurs as if in sleep. She notices the food tray by the bed, and snatches it up: returns to* THE WITCH, *downstage.*]

MRS GOFORTH: He's already making long-distance calls on the phone and look at this. He's had them bring him a food tray and I am going to remove it. I can't stand guests, especially not invited, that act like they're in a hotel, charging calls and calling for room service. Come on, I'm turning out the lights.

THE WITCH: My slippers.

> [*She slips back to the bed and picks up her slippers: lingers over* CHRIS: *suddenly bends to kiss him on the mouth. He rolls over quickly, shielding his lower face with an arm and uttering a grunt of distaste.*]

Possum!

> [*The lights dim in the area: as* THE WITCH *moves downstage:* MRS GOFORTH *has disappeared.*]

Sissy? Sissy? Yoo-hoo!

MRS GOFORTH [*at a distance*]: Yoo-hoo!

THE WITCH [*crossing into the wings*]: Yooooooooo-hoooooo . . .

[*The* STAGE ASSISTANTS *replace the screen that masked the pink villa bed. Then they fold and remove the screen before* BLACKIE's *bed in the blue villa.*

The area remains dark till a faint dawn light appears on the cyclorama. Then BLACKIE's *bed is lighted and we see her seated on it, brushing her dark hair with a silver-backed brush.*]

Scene Four

Later that night: the terrace of the white villa. The watchman RUDY sweeps the audience with the beam of his flashlight. We hear a long, anguished 'Ahhh' from behind the screen masking MRS GOFORTH's bed. RUDY, as if he heard the outcry, turns the flashlight momentarily on the screen behind which it comes. He chuckles: sways drunkenly: then suddenly turns the light beam on the figure of CHRIS who has entered quietly from the wings, stage right.

CHRIS [*shielding his eyes from the flashlight*]: Oh. Hello.

RUDY: You still prowling around here?

CHRIS [*still agreeably*]: No, I'm. Well, yes, I'm – [*His smile fades as RUDY moves in closer.*] – I just now woke up hungry. I didn't want to disturb anybody, so I –

RUDY: You just now woke up, huh?

CHRIS: Yes, I –

RUDY: Where'd you just now wake up?

CHRIS: In the, uh, guest-house, the –

RUDY: Looking for the dogs again, are you? [*Whistles the dogs awake. They set up a clamour at a distance.*]

CHRIS: I told you I just now woke up hungry: I came out to see if –

RUDY [*moving still closer and cutting in*]: Aw, you woke up *hungry*?

CHRIS: Yes. Famished.

RUDY: How about this, how'd you like to eat this, something like this, huh? [*Thrusts his stick hard into CHRIS's stomach.*]

CHRIS: [*Expels his breath in a 'hah'.*]

RUDY: 'Sthat feel good on your belly? Want some more of that, huh?

[*Drives the stick again into CHRIS's stomach, so hard that CHRIS bends over, unable to speak.* BLACKIE *rushes on to the terrace in a dressing-gown, her hair loose.*]

BLACKIE: RUDY! WHAT'S GOING ON HERE?

[*The* DOGS *have roused and have started barking at a distance.*]

This young man is a guest of Mrs Goforth. He's staying in the pink villa. Are you all right, Mr Flanders?

[CHRIS *can't speak: leans on a section of balustrade, bent over, making a retching sound.*]

Rudy, get off the terrace! – you drunk gorilla!

RUDY: [*grinning*]: He's got the dry heaves, Blackie, he woke up hungry and he's got the dry heaves.

CHRIS: *Can't – catch – breath!*

[*From her bed behind the griffin-crested screen,* MRS GOFORTH *cries out in her sleep, a long, anguished 'Ahhhhhh!'.*

DOG *barking subsides gradually. The 'Ahhhhh' is repeated and a faint light appears behind her screen.* BLACKIE *turns on* RUDY, *fiercely.*]

BLACKIE: I said get off the terrace, now get off it.

RUDY: You shoulda told me you –

BLACKIE: Off it, off the terrace!

RUDY [*overlapping*]: You got yourself a boy-friend up here, Blackie! You should've let me know that.

BLACKIE: Mr Flanders, I'll take you back to your place.

CHRIS [*gaspingly*]: Is there – anywhere closer – I could catch my breath?

BLACKIE: Yes. Yes, I'll – my place is closer . . .

[*She stands protectively near him as* RUDY *goes off the terrace, laughing.*

The STAGE ASSISTANTS *rush out to remove a screen masking* BLACKIE's *bed in the blue villa, announcing 'Blackie's bedroom'.* CHRIS *straightens slowly, still gasping. The* STAGE ASSISTANTS *exit.*

Then CHRIS *and* BLACKIE *cross to her villino, represented only by a narrow blue-sheeted bed with a stand beside it that supports an inter-com. box.*]

BLACKIE: Now tell me just what happened so I can give a report to Mrs Goforth tomorrow.

CHRIS: The truth is I was looking for something to eat. I've had no food for five days, Blackie, except some oranges that I picked on the road. And you know what the acid, the citric acid in oranges, does to an empty stomach, so I – I woke up feeling as if I had a – a bushel of burning sawdust in my stomach, and I –

BLACKIE: I had food sent to your room, you didn't find it?

CHRIS: No. God, no!

BLACKIE: Then the cook didn't send it or it was taken out while you were sleeping, and I'm afraid you'll have to wait till morning for something to eat. You see the only kitchen is in Mrs Goforth's villa, it's locked up like a bank vault till Mrs Goforth wakes up and has it opened.

CHRIS: How long is it till morning?

BLACKIE: Oh, my – watch has stopped. I'm a watch-winding person but I forgot to wind it.

[*The cyclorama has lightened a little and there is the sound of church-bells at a distance.*]

CHRIS: The church-bells are waking up on the other mountains.

BLACKIE: Yes, it's, it must be near morning, but morning doesn't begin on Mrs Goforth's mountain till she sleeps off her drugs and starts pressing buttons for the sun to come up. So –

CHRIS: – What?

[*The inter-com. box comes alive with a shrill electric buzz.*]

BLACKIE: Oh, God, she's awake, buzzing for me!

CHRIS: Oh, then, could you ask her to open the kitchen? A glass of milk, just some milk, is all I –

BLACKIE: Mrs Goforth isn't buzzing for morning, she's buzzing for me to take dictation and, Oh, God, I don't think I can do it. I haven't slept tonight and I just couldn't take it right now, I –

CHRIS: Let me take it for you.

BLACKIE: No. I'll have to answer myself or she'll come stumbling raving out and might fall off the cliff. [*She presses a button on the inter-com. box.*] Mrs Goforth? Mrs Goforth?

[*The* STAGE ASSISTANTS *remove the screen masking* MRS GO-FORTH*'s bed, up stage left. We see her through the gauze curtains enclosing the bed. She pulls a cord opening the curtains and speaks hoarsely into a microphone.*]

MRS GOFORTH: *Blackie? It's night, late night!*

BLACKIE: Yes, it's late, Mrs Goforth.

MRS GOFORTH: Don't answer: this is dictation. Don't interrupt me, this is clear as a vision. The death of Harlon Goforth, just now – clearly – remembered, clear as a vision. It's night, late night, without sleep. He's crushing me under the awful weight of his body. Then suddenly he stops trying to make love to me. He says, Flora, I have a pain in my head, a terrible pain in my head. And silently to myself, I say, Thank God, but out loud I say something else: 'Tablets, you want your tablets?' He answers with the groan of – I reach up and turn on the light, and I see – death in his eyes! I see, I know. He has death in his eyes, and something worse in them, terror. I see terror in his eyes. I see it, I feel it, myself, and I get out of the bed, I get out of the bed as if escaping from quicksand! I don't look at him again, I move away from the bed . . .

[*We see her rising from the bed, the microphone gripped in her hand.*]

I move away from death, terror! I don't look back, I go straight to the door, the door on to the terrace! [*She moves downstage with the microphone.*] It's closed, I tear it open, I leave him alone with his death, his –

BLACKIE: She's out of bed, she's going out on the – [*She rushes into the wings: light dims on the blue villa bed.*]

MRS GOFORTH [*dropping the microphone as she moves out on the white villa terrace*]: I've gone out, now, I'm outside, I'm on the terrace, twenty-five stories over the high, high city of Goforth, I see lights blazing as bright as the blaze of terror that I saw in his eyes! [*She staggers to the edge of the forestage.*] Wind, cold wind, clean, clean! Release! Relief! Escape from – [*She reaches the edges of the orchestra pit. A wave crashes loudly below.*] I'm lost, blind, dying! I don't know where I –

BLACKIE [*rushing out behind her*]: Mrs Goforth! Don't move! You're at the edge of the cliff!

MRS GOFORTH [*stopping, her hands over her eyes*]: Blackie! [*She sways: BLACKIE rushes forward to catch her.*] Blackie, don't leave me alone!

THE STAGE IS BLACKED OUT: INTERMISSION

Scene Five

The terrace of the white villa the following morning: MRS GOFORTH *is standing on the terrace while dictating to* BLACKIE, *who sits at a small table. Above the table and about the balustrade are cascades of bougainvillaea: coins of gold light, reflected from the sea far below, flicker upon the playing area, which is backed by fair sky. There has been a long, reflective pause in the dictation.*

MRS GOFORTH *stands glaring sombrely out at the sea.*

MRS GOFORTH: *Blackie, I want to begin this chapter on a more serious note.* [*She moves around right of the table. Then emphatically and loudly.*] MEANING OF LIFE!

BLACKIE: Dictation?

MRS GOFORTH: Not yet, wait, don't rush me. [*Repeats in a softer tone: 'meaning of Life . . .'*]

[CHRIS *appears at a far end of the terrace. He wears the Samurai robe.* BLACKIE *sees him but* MRS GOFORTH *doesn't:* BLACKIE *indicates by gesture that he should not approach yet.*]

Yes, I feel this chapter ought to begin with a serious comment on the meaning of life, because, y'know, sooner or later, a person's obliged to face it.

BLACKIE: Dictating, now, Mrs Goforth?

MRS GOFORTH: No, no, thinking – reflecting, I'll raise my hand when I begin the dictation.

[*She raises a jewelled hand to demonstrate the signal that she will use.*]

BLACKIE: Begin now?

> [CHRIS *smiles at her tone of voice:* BLACKIE *shrugs and closes her notebook: rises quietly and goes up to* CHRIS *for a smoke.*]

MRS GOFORTH: One time at Flora's Folly which was the name of the sixteenth-century coach-house, renovated, near Paris where I had my salon, my literary evenings, I brought up that question, 'What is the meaning of Life?' And do you know they treated it like a joke? Ha ha, very funny, Sissy can't be serious! – but she *was*, she *was* . . .

CHRIS: I think she's started dictating. Is there something to eat?

BLACKIE: Black coffee and saccharine tablets.

CHRIS: That's *all*?!

BLACKIE: Soon as I get a chance I'll raid the kitchen for you.

MRS GOFORTH [*almost plaintively*]: Why is it considered ridiculous, bad taste, *mauvais goût*, to seriously consider and discuss the possible meaning of life and only stylish to assume it's just – what?

> [*The* STAGE ASSISTANTS *have come out of the wings.*]

ONE: Charade. Game.

TWO [*tossing a spangled ball to his partner*]: Pastime.

ONE [*tossing the ball back*]: Flora's Folly.

ONE [*same action*]: Accident of atoms.

TWO [*same action*]: Resulting from indiscriminate copulation.

> [BLACKIE *tosses her cigarette away and returns to her former position. The* STAGE ASSISTANTS *withdraw.*]

MRS GOFORTH: I've often wondered but I've wondered *more* lately: meaning of *life*.

> [*The* STAGE ASSISTANTS *reappear with a small table and two chairs: wait in the wings for the moment to place them.*]

– Sometimes I think, I suspect, that everything that we do is a way of – *not* thinking about it. Meaning of life, and meaning of death, too . . . WHAT IN HELL ARE WE DOING? [*Raises her jewelled hand.*] Just going from one goddam frantic distraction to another, till finally one too many goddam frantic distractions leads to disaster, and black out? Eclipse of, total of, sun? [*She keeps staring out from the terrace, her head turning slowly right and left, into the swimming gold light below her, murmuring to herself, nodding a little, then shaking her head a little: her small jewelled hands appear to be groping blindly for something: she coughs from time to time.*] – There's a fog coming in. See it over there, that fog coming in?

BLACKIE: No. It's perfectly clear in all directions this morning.

MRS GOFORTH: When I woke up this morning, I said to myself –

BLACKIE: Dictation?

MRS GOFORTH: Shut up – I said to myself, Oh, God, not morning again, oh, no, no, I can't bear it. But I *did*, I bore it. – You really don't see that mist coming in out there?

BLACKIE [*closing her notebook*]: – Mrs Goforth, the young man in the pink villa, Mr Flanders, is waiting out here to see you. He has on the Samurai robe you gave him to wear while his clothes are being repaired and it's very becoming to him.

MRS GOFORTH: Call him over.

BLACKIE: Mr Flanders!

MRS GOFORTH: Hay, Samurai! *Bonzei!*

[*Approaching, he ducks under a brilliant cascade of bougainvillaea vine.*]

BLACKIE: You certainly had a long sleep.

CHRIS: Did I ever!

MRS GOFORTH: DID he ever, ho ho. He slept round the clock but still has romantic shadows under his eyes! There was a chorus girl in the Follies – I used to be in the Follies, before my first marriage – when she'd show up with circles under her eyes, she'd say, 'The blackbirds kissed me last night' meaning she's been too busy to sleep that night, ho ho . . .

CHRIS: I was busy sleeping, just sleeping. [*He bends over her hand.*]

MRS GOFORTH: No, no, none of that stuff. Old Georgia swamp-bitches don't go in for hand-kissing but – setzen sie doon, and – Are you coming out here for battle with that sword on?

CHRIS: Oh. No, but – I ran into a pack of wild dogs on the mountain, yesterday, when I climbed up here.

MRS GOFORTH: Yes, I heard about your little misunderstanding with the dogs. You don't seem much the worse for it. You're lucky they didn't get at – [*grins wickedly*] – your *face*.

CHRIS: I'm sorry if it disturbed you, but their bite was worse than their bark.

MRS GOFORTH: The Italians call them Lupos which means wolves, these watchdogs: they're necessary for the protection of estates like this, but – didn't you notice the 'Private Property' sign in English and Italian, and the 'Beware of Dogs' sign when you started up that goat-path from the highway?

CHRIS: I don't think I noticed a reference to dogs, no, I don't remember any mention of dogs, in English or Italian.

BLACKIE [*quickly*]: Naturally not, the 'Beware of Dogs' sign was put up *after* Mr Flanders' 'little misunderstanding with the dogs'.

MRS GOFORTH: Blackie, that is not so.

BLACKIE: Yes, it *is* so, I heard you ordering the sign put up after, just after the –

MRS GOFORTH [*trembling with fury*]: Blackie! You have *work* to do, don't you?

BLACKIE: I've never taken a job that called for collusion in – falsehood!

MRS GOFORTH [*mocking her*]: Oh, what virtue, what high moral character, Blackie.

CHRIS [*cutting in quickly*]: Mrs Goforth, Miss Black, I obviously *did* enter and trespass on private property at my own risk.

MRS GOFORTH: If that statement's typed up – Blackie, type it up. – Would you be willing to sign it, Mr Flanders?

CHRIS: Certainly, yes, of course, but let me write it up in my own handwriting and sign it right now. I'd hate for you to think I'd –

BLACKIE: He was attacked again last night.

MRS GOFORTH: Again, by dogs?

BLACKIE: Not by dogs, by a dog, your watchman, Rudy, attacked him because he woke up hungry and came outside to –

MRS GOFORTH [*rising*]: BLACKIE, GET OFF THE TERRACE!

BLACKIE: I want to get off this mountain gone mad with your madness! I try to help you, I try to feel sorry for you because you're –

MRS GOFORTH: WHAT? WHAT AM I?

CHRIS: Please. [*Tears a page out of* BLACKIE'S *notebook and says to her quietly.*] It's all right. Go in.

MRS GOFORTH: What did you say to that woman?

CHRIS: I said you're very upset, I said you're trembling.

MRS GOFORTH: *I've been up here surrounded by traitors all summer!* [*Staggers.*] *Ahhhhh!*

[*He helps her into her chair.*]

– God! God . . .

CHRIS: Now. [*Scribbles rapidly on the sheet of paper.*] Here. 'I, Christopher Flanders, entered a gate marked Private at my own risk and am solely responsible for a – misunderstanding with – dogs.' – Witnesses? Of the signature?

MRS GOFORTH: Can you unscrew this bottle? [*She has been trying to open her codeine bottle.*]

CHRIS [*taking it from her and removing the cap*]: One?

MRS GOFORTH: Two. – Thank you. – Brandy on that –

[*Indicates liquor cart.*]

CHRIS: Courvoisier?

MRS GOFORTH: Rémy-Martin. – Thank you.

CHRIS: Welcome. [*He resumes his seat and smiles at her warmly.*] Let me hold that glass for you.

[*She has spilled some of the brandy, her hand is shaking so violently.*]

MRS GOFORTH: Thank you.

[*He sits back down and resumes his smile, with a quick, friendly nod.*]

– Ahh . . . [*Draws a deep breath: begins to recover herself.*] – You have nice teeth. – Are they capped?

[CHRIS *shakes his head, smiling more.*]

Well, you got beautiful teeth, in that respect nature's been favourable to you.

CHRIS: Thank you.

MRS GOFORTH: Don't thank me, thank your dentist. [*She's putting on lipstick and dabbing her nostrils with a bit of disposable tissue.*]

CHRIS: I've never been to a dentist: honestly not.

MRS GOFORTH: Well, then, thank the Lord for the calcium that you got from your mother's milk. Well, I have a pretty wonderful set of teeth myself. In fact, my teeth are so good people think they are false. But look, look here! [*She takes her large incisors between thumb and forefinger to demonstrate the firmness of their attachment.*] See? Not even a bridge. – In my whole mouth I've had exactly three fillings which are still there, put in there ten years ago! See them? [*She opens her mouth wide to expose its interior to him.*] – This tooth here was slightly chipped when my daughter's third baby struck me in the mouth with the butt of a water pistol at Murray Bay. I told my daughter that girl would turn into a problem child and it sure as hell did. – A little pocket-size bitch, getting bigger! I'm allergic to bitches. Although some people regard me as one myself . . . Sometimes *with* some justification. Want some coffee, Mr Trojan Horse Guest?

CHRIS: Thanks, yes: – why do you call me that, a Trojan Horse Guest?

MRS GOFORTH: Because you've arrived here without invitation, like the Trojan Horse got into Troy. [*She has risen shakily to pour him a cup of coffee from a silver urn on the smaller upstage table.*]

CHRIS: Don't you remember our meeting and conversation at the Ballet Ball, some years ago, quite a few when you asked me to come whenever I was in Europe?

MRS GOFORTH: Passports expire and so do invitations. They've got to be renewed every couple of years.

CHRIS: Has my invitation expired?

MRS GOFORTH: Coffee. We'll see about that, that remains to be seen.

[NOTE: *While she was pouring the coffee, he may have quietly crumpled the sheet of paper and thrown it into the orchestra pit, such an action being in line with the ambiguity of his character.*]

Don't you smoke with your coffee?

CHRIS: Usually, but I –

[*He indicates he has no cigarettes.* MRS GOFORTH *smiles knowingly and opens a cigarette box on the table.*]

CHRIS: How does it feel, Mrs Goforth, to be a legend in your own lifetime?

MRS GOFORTH [*pleased*]: If that's a serious question. I'll give it a serious answer. A legend in my own lifetime, yes, I reckon I am. Well, I had certain advantages, endowments to start with, a face people naturally noticed and a figure that was not just sensational, but very durable, too. Some women my age, or younger, 've got breasts that look like a couple of mules hangin' their heads over the top rail of a fence. [*Touches her bosom.*] This is natural, not padded, not supported: and nothing's ever been lifted. Hell, I was born between a swamp and the wrong side of the tracks in One Street, Georgia, but not even that could stop me in my tracks, wrong side or right side or no side. Hit show-biz at fifteen when a carnival show, I mean the manager of it, saw me and dug me on that One Street in One Street, Georgia. I was billed as the Dixie Doxey, was just supposed to move my anatomy but was smart enough to keep my tongue moving, too, and the verbal comments I made on my anatomical motions while in motion were a public delight. So I breezed through show-biz like a tornado, rising from one-week 'gigs' in the sticks to star-billing in 'The Follies' while still in m'teens, ho ho . . . and I was still in my teens when I married Harlon Goforth, a marriage into the Social Register and Dun-and-Bradstreet's, both. Was barely out of my teens when I became his widow. Scared to make out a will, he died intestate so everything went to me.

CHRIS: Marvellous. Amazing.

MRS GOFORTH: That's right, all my life was and still *is* except here lately I'm a little run-down, like a race-horse that's been entered in just one race too many, even for me . . . How do *you* feel about being a legend in your own lifetime? Huh?

CHRIS: Oh, *me!* I don't feel like a – mythological – griffin with gold wings, but this strong fresh wind's reviving me like I'd had a – terrific breakfast!

MRS GOFORTH: Griffin, what's a griffin?

CHRIS: A force in life that's almost stronger than death. [*Springs up, turns to the booming sea.*] The sea's full of white race-horses today. May I, would you mind if I, suggested a programme for us? A picnic on the beach, rest on the rocks in the sun till nearly sundown, then we'd come back up here revitalized for whatever the lovely evening had to offer?

MRS GOFORTH: What do you think it would have to offer?

CHRIS: Dinner on the terrace with the sea still booming? How is that for a programme? Say, with music, a couple of tarantella dancers brought up from the village, and –

[RUDY *appears on the terrace.*]

RUDY: Miss Goforth, I've taken care of that for you, they're going, on the way out.

MRS GOFORTH: No trouble?

RUDY: Oh, yeah, sure, they want to see the Signora.

MRS GOFORTH: No, no, no. I won't see them!

[*But 'they' are appearing upstage: her* KITCHEN STAFF *discharged.*]

Here they come, hold them back!

[*She staggers up, turns her back on them. They cry out to her in Italian.* RUDY *rushes upstage and herds them violently off. A wave crashes.*]

CHRIS [*quietly*]: Boom. – What was their –?

MRS GOFORTH: What?

CHRIS: – Transgression?

MRS GOFORTH: They'd been robbing me blind, he caught them at it, we had – an inventory and discovered that – they'd been robbing me blind like I was – blind . . .

CHRIS [*his back to her, speaking as if to himself*]: When a wave breaks down there, it looks as delicate as a white lace fan, but I bet if it hit you, it would knock you against the rocks and break your bones . . .

MRS GOFORTH: What?

CHRIS: – I said it's so wonderful here, after yesterday in Naples . . .

MRS GOFORTH: What was wrong with yesterday in Naples? Were you picked up for vagrancy in Naples?

CHRIS: I wasn't picked up for anything in Naples.

MRS GOFORTH: That's worse than being picked up for vagrancy, baby. [*She chuckles: he grins agreeably*.]

CHRIS: Mrs Goforth, I'm going to tell you the truth.

MRS GOFORTH: The truth is all you could tell me that I'd believe so tell me the truth, Mr Flanders.

CHRIS: I'll go back a little further than Naples, Mrs Goforth. I'd drawn out all my savings account to come over here this summer on a Yugoslavian freighter that landed at Genoa.

MRS GOFORTH: You're leading up to financial troubles, aren't you?

CHRIS: Not so much that as – something harder, much harder, for me to deal with, a state of – Well, let me put it this way. Everybody has a sense of *reality* of some kind or other, some kind of sense of things being real or not real in his, his – particular – world . . .

MRS GOFORTH: I know what you mean: go on.

CHRIS: I've lost it lately: this sense of reality in my particular world. We don't all live in the same world, you know, Mrs Goforth, oh, we all see the same things – sea, sun, sky, human faces and inhuman faces, but – they're different in *here*! [*Touches his forehead*.] And one person's sense of reality can be another person's sense of – Well, of madness! – Chaos! – And, and –

MRS GOFORTH: Go on: I'm still with you.

CHRIS: And when one person's sense of reality, or loss of sense of reality, disturbs another one's sense of reality – I know how mixed up this –

MRS GOFORTH: Not a bit, clear as a bell, so keep on, y'haven't lost my attention.

CHRIS: Being able to talk: wonderful! – When one person's sense of reality seems too – disturbingly different from another person's, uh –

MRS GOFORTH: Sense of reality: Continue.

CHRIS: Well, he's – avoided! Not welcome! It's – *that simple* . . . And – yesterday in Naples, I suddenly realized that I was in that situation. [*Turns to the booming sea and says 'Boom'.*] I found out that I was now a – *leper!*

MRS GOFORTH: Leopard?

CHRIS: LEPER! – BOOM!

[*She ignores the 'boom'.*]

Yes, you see, they hang labels, tags of false identification, on people that disturb their own sense of reality too much, like the bells that used to be hung on the necks of – *lepers!* – BOOM!

– The lady I'd come over to visit who lives in a castle on the top of Ravello, sent me a wire to Naples. I walked to Naples on foot to pick it up, and picked it up at American Express in Naples, and what it said was: 'Not yet, not ready for you, dear – Angel of – Death . . .'

[MRS GOFORTH *regards him a bit uncomfortably. He smiles very warmly at her, she relaxes.*]

MRS GOFORTH: – Ridiculous!

CHRIS: Yes, and inconvenient since I'd –

MRS GOFORTH: Invested all your remaining capital in this standing invitation that had stopped standing, collapsed, ho, ho, ho!

CHRIS: – Yes . . .

MRS GOFORTH: Who's this bitch at Ravello?

CHRIS: I'd rather forget her name, now.

MRS GOFORTH: But you see you young people, well, you *reasonably* young people who used to be younger, you get in the habit of being sort of – professional house-guests, and as you get a bit older, and who doesn't get a bit older, some more than just a *bit* older, you're still professional house-guests, and –

CHRIS: Yes?

MRS GOFORTH: Oh, you have charm, all of you, you still have your good looks and charm and you all do something creative, such as writing but not writing and painting but not painting, and that goes fine for a time but –

CHRIS: You've made your point, Mrs Goforth.

MRS GOFORTH: No, not yet, quite yet. Your case is special. You've gotten a special nickname, 'Dear Angel of Death'. – And it's lucky for you I couldn't be less superstitious, deliberately walk under ladders, think a black cat's as lucky as a white cat, am only against the human cats of this world of which there's no small number. So! What're you looking around for, Angel of Death, as they call you?

CHRIS: I would love to have some buttered toast with my coffee.

MRS GOFORTH: Oh, no toast with my coffee, buttered, unbuttered, no toast. For breakfast I have only black coffee. Anything solid takes the edge off my energy and it's the time after breakfast when I do my best work.

CHRIS: What are you working on?

MRS GOFORTH: My memories, my memoirs, night and day, to meet the publishers' deadlines. The pressure has brought on a sort of nervous breakdown, and I'm enjoying every minute of it because it has taken the form of making me absolutely frank and honest with people, no more pretences, although I was always frank and honest with people: comparatively: but now much more so. No more pretences at all . . .

CHRIS: It's wonderful.

MRS GOFORTH: What?

CHRIS: That you and I have happened to meet at just this time because I have reached the same point in my life as you say you have come to in yours.

MRS GOFORTH [*suspiciously*]: What? Which? Point?

CHRIS: The point you mentioned, the point of no more pretences.

MRS GOFORTH: You say you've reached that point, too?

[CHRIS *nods, smiling warmly.*]

Hmmmm.

[*The sound is sceptical and so is the look she gives him.*]

CHRIS: It's *true*, I *have*, Mrs Goforth.

MRS GOFORTH: I don't mean to call you a liar or even a fantasist, but I don't see how you could afford to arrive at the point of no more pretences, Chris.

CHRIS: I probably couldn't afford to arrive at this point any more than I could afford to travel this summer.

MRS GOFORTH: Hmmm. I see. But you travelled?

CHRIS: Yes, mostly on foot, Mrs Goforth – since – Genoa.

MRS GOFORTH [*rises and crosses near balustrade*]: One of the reasons I took this place here is because it's supposed to be inaccessible except from the sea. Between here and the highway, there's just a goat-path, hardly possible to get down, and I thought impossible to get up. Hmmm. Yes. Well. But you got yourself up.

CHRIS [*pours last of the coffee*]: I had to. I had to get up it.

MRS GOFORTH [*crossing back to him and sitting*]: Let's play the truth game: do you know the truth game?

CHRIS: Yes, but I don't like it. I've always made excuses to get out of it when it's played at parties because I think the truth is too delicate and, well, *dangerous* a thing to be played with at parties, Mrs Goforth. It's nitro-glycerine, it has to be handled with the – the carefulest care, or somebody hurts somebody and gets hurt back and the party turns to a – devastating explosion, people crying, people screaming, people even fighting and throwing things at each other. I've seen it happen, and there's no truth in it – that's true.

MRS GOFORTH: But you say you've reached the same point that I have this summer, the point of no more pretences, so why can't we play the truth game together, huh, Chris?

CHRIS: – Why don't we put it off till – say, after – supper?

MRS GOFORTH: You play it better on a full stomach, do you?

CHRIS: Yes, you have to be physically fortified for it as well as – morally fortified for it.

MRS GOFORTH: And you like to stay for supper? You don't have any other engagement for supper?

CHRIS: I have no engagements of any kind now, Mrs Goforth.

MRS GOFORTH: Well, I don't know about supper. Sometimes I don't want any.

CHRIS: How about after –?

MRS GOFORTH: – What?

CHRIS: After lunch?

MRS GOFORTH: Oh, sometimes I don't have lunch, either.

CHRIS: You're not on a healthful régime. You know, the spirit has to live in the body and so you have to keep the body in a state of repair because it's the home of the – spirit . . .

MRS GOFORTH: – Hmmm. Are you talking about your spirit and body or mine?

CHRIS: Yours.

MRS GOFORTH: One long ago meeting between us, and you expect me to believe you care more about my spirit and body than your own? Mr Flanders?

CHRIS: Mrs Goforth, some people, some people, most of them, get panicky when they're not cared for by somebody, but I get panicky when I have no one to care for.

MRS GOFORTH: Oh, you seem to be setting yourself up as a – as a saint of some kind . . .

CHRIS: All I said is I need somebody to care for. I don't say that – [*He has finished his coffee and crosses to the warmer for more.*] I'm playing the truth game with you. Caring for somebody gives me the sense of being – sheltered, protected . . .

MRS GOFORTH: 'Sheltered, protected' from what?

CHRIS [*standing above her*]: – Unreality! – lostness? – Have you ever seen how two little animals sleep together, a pair of kittens or puppies? All day they seem so secure in the house of their master, but at night, when they sleep, they don't seem sure of their owner's true care for them: then they draw close together: they curl up against each other, and now and then, if you watch them, you notice they nudge each other a little with their heads or their paws, exchange little signals between them. The signals mean: we're not in danger . . . sleep: we're close: – it's safe here. – Their owner's house is never a sure protection, a reliable shelter. – Everything going on in it is mysterious to them, and no matter how hard they try to please, how do they know if they please? – They hear so many sounds, voices, and see so many things they can't comprehend! – Oh, it's ever so much better than the pet shop window but what's become of their mother? – who warmed them and sheltered them and fed them until they were snatched away from her, for no reason they know. We're all of us living in a house we're not used to – too . . . A house full of – voices, noises, objects, strange shadows, light that's even stranger – we can't understand. We bark and jump around and try to – be – *pleasingly playful* in this big mysterious house but – in our hearts we're all very frightened of it: don't you think so? – Then it gets to be dark. – We're left alone with each other: we have to creep close to each other and give those gentle little nudges with our paws and our muzzles before we can slip into – sleep and – rest for the next day's – playtime . . . and the next day's mysteries. [*He lights a cigarette for her as* THE WITCH *enters dramatically still on terrace.*]

THE WITCH: The next day's mysteries. Ecco, sono qui.

MRS GOFORTH: My Lord, are you still here? [*With unconcealed displeasure.* CHRIS *turns.*]

THE WITCH [*as if amazed*]: Christopher! Flanders!

CHRIS: How do you do, Mrs – Oh, I started to say Mrs Ridgeway but that isn't it, now, is it?

THE WITCH: What a back number you are!

[*He draws back from her and crosses away.*]

CHRIS: Yes.

MRS GOFORTH: How'd you miss your return trip to Capri last night, I thought you'd gone back there last night? I had the boatman waiting up for you last night.

THE WITCH: Oh, last night! What confusion! [*She puts down her hat and follows* CHRIS.] When was the last time I saw you?

MRS GOFORTH: If you don't know why should he?

THE WITCH: Oh, at the wedding banquet those Texas oil people gave me in Portofino, oh, yes, you were staying with them, and so depressed over the loss of –

CHRIS [*cutting in*]: Yes. [*He moves again toward the balustrade.*]

THE WITCH: You'd taken such beautiful care of that poor old ridiculous woman but couldn't save her, and, oh, the old Duke of Parma did such a wicked thing to you, poured champagne on your head and – called you – what did he call you?

MRS GOFORTH: Let him forget it, Connie.

[THE WITCH *gives her a glance and moves to* CHRIS.]

THE WITCH: Something else awful happened and you were involved in some way but I can't remember the details.

CHRIS: Yes, it's better forgotten, Mrs Goforth is right, some of the details are much better forgotten if you'll let me – forget them . . .

[MRS GOFORTH *rises and starts upstage.*]

THE WITCH: Are you leaving us, Sissy?

MRS GOFORTH: I'm going to phone the boat-house t'make sure there's a boat ready for your trip back to Capri, because I know you want back there soon as possible, Connie. [*She crosses into the library and out the door.*]

THE WITCH [*crossing now to the table*]: Chris, you're not intending to STAY here!?

CHRIS: Yes, if I'm invited: I would like to.

THE WITCH: Don't you know, can't you tell? Poor Sissy's going, she's gone. The shock I got last night when I – I had to drink myself blind! – when I saw her condition! [*She crosses closer.*] You don't want to be stuck with a person in her appalling condition. You're young, have fun. Oh, Chris, you've been foolish too long, the years you devoted to that old Ferguson bitch, and what did you get?

CHRIS [*lighting a cigarette*]: Get?

THE WITCH: Yes, get? She *had* you, you were *had!* – *left* you? *Nothing!* – I bet, or why would you be here?

CHRIS: Please don't make me be rude: we don't understand each other, which is natural, but don't make me say things to you that I don't want to say.

THE WITCH: What can you say to me that I haven't heard said?

CHRIS: Have you heard this said to your face about you, that you're the heart of a world that has no heart, the heartless world you live in, has anyone said that to you, Mrs Ridgeway?

THE WITCH: Condotti, Marchesa Ridgeway-Condotti, Mr Death Angel Flanders.

CHRIS: Yes, we both have new titles.

THE WITCH [*throwing back her head*]: Sally! Laurie! Sissy! It's time for death, old girls, beddy-bye! [*Less shrilly*] Beddy-bye, old girls, the Death Angel's coming, no dreams . . .

[*Meanwhile in the library area:* MRS GOFORTH *enters, followed by* BLACKIE *with a notebook.*]

MRS GOFORTH: Ah, God . . . What in Hell's going on here?

BLACKIE: I wish I knew, Mrs Goforth.

MRS GOFORTH [*circling the desk*]: I call, I buzz, no one answers!

BLACKIE: I was in the kitchen when you –

MRS GOFORTH: Why in the kitchen?

BLACKIE: The new kitchen staff had arrived and I was explaining the kitchen equipment to them.

MRS GOFORTH [*cutting in*]: Never mind that, let that go, just call the boat-house and have them have a boat ready to take the Capri Witch back to Capri.

[BLACKIE *moves to phone.*]

She's still here, spent the night here. Why didn't you get her away when – Look! Look!

[THE WITCH *has crossed toward* CHRIS, *who turns.*]

CHRIS: I'm sorry you forced me to say what I feel about you.

THE WITCH: Oh, that. My heart pumps blood that isn't my own blood, it's the blood of anonymous blood donors, and as for the world I live in, you know it as well as I know it. – Come to Capri, it's a mountain, too.

CHRIS [*again moving away*]: You're not afraid of the nickname I've been given?

THE WITCH: No, I think it's a joke that you take seriously, Chris. You've gotten too solemn. [*She follows him.*] Let me take that curse off you. Come to Capri, and I'll give you a party, decorated with your mobiles, and –

MRS GOFORTH [*to* BLACKIE]: See? She's out there putting the make on –

[BLACKIE *exits as* MRS GOFORTH *crosses out of the library.*]

THE WITCH [*cutting into* MRS GOFORTH'*s speech*]: You're pale, you look anaemic, you look famished, you need someone to put you back in the picture, the social swim. Capri?

[MRS GOFORTH *has come back out on the terrace: she advances behind* CHRIS *and* THE WITCH.]

MRS GOFORTH: What picture? What swim? Capri?

THE WITCH: It's marvellous there this season.

MRS GOFORTH: The sea is full of Medusas. Didn't you tell me the sea is full of Medusas and a giant one got you?

THE WITCH [*crossing to her*]: Oh, they'll wash out, they'll be washed out by tomorrow.

MRS GOFORTH: When are *you* going to wash out? I thought you'd washed out last night – I've ordered a boat to take you back to Capri.

THE WITCH: I can't go back to Capri in a dinner gown before sundown. [*She sits at the table and stares at* CHRIS.]

MRS GOFORTH: Well, try my hot sulphur baths or just look the place over, it's worth it. It's worth looking over. Me, I'm about to start work so I can't talk to you right now. [*She gets* THE WITCH*'s hat and brings it to her.*] I'm right on the edge of breaking through here today, I'm on a strict discipline, Connie, as I explained last night to you, and – [*She coughs: falls into her chair.*]

THE WITCH: Sissy, I don't like that cough.

MRS GOFORTH: Hell, do you think I like it? Neuralgia, nerves, over-work, but I'm going to beat it, it isn't going to beat *me* or it'll be the first thing that ever *did* beat me!

THE WITCH [*rising and crossing to her*]: Be brave, Sissy – 'Snothing more necessary.

MRS GOFORTH: Leave me alone, go, Connie, it'll do you in, too. [*She crosses away for a tissue.* THE WITCH *looks, wide-eyed, at* CHRIS *and crosses to him.*]

THE WITCH: Watch out for each other! – Chris, give her the Swami's book you translated. Ciao! [*She throws him a kiss and moves off, calling back.*] *Qu'este veramente* una meraviglia . . . – *Ciao, arrivederci . . . Amici!* [THE WITCH *goes out of the lighted area down the goat-path.* CHRIS *crosses to table and sits, looking about.*]

MRS GOFORTH: What are you looking for now?

CHRIS: I was just looking for the cream and sugar.

MRS GOFORTH: Never touch it, y'want a saccharine tablet?

CHRIS: Oh, no, thanks, I – don't like the chemical taste.

MRS GOFORTH [*crossing down to table*]: Well, it's black coffee or else, I'm afraid, Mr what? – Chris!

CHRIS: You have *three* villas here?

MRS GOFORTH: One villa and two villinos. Villino means a small villa. I also have a little grass hut, very Polynesian – [*Crossing a little below the table.*] down on my private beach too. I have a special use for it, and a funny name for it, too.

CHRIS: Oh?

MRS GOFORTH: Yes, I call it 'The Oubliette'. Ever heard of the Oubliette?

CHRIS: A place where people are put to be forgotten?

MRS GOFORTH: That's right, Chris. You've had some education along that line. [*She crosses above the table, closer to him.*]

CHRIS: Yes, quite a lot, Mrs Goforth, especially lately.

MRS GOFORTH: As for the use of it, well, I've been plagued by imposters lately, the last few summers, the continent has been overrun by imposters of celebrities, writers, actors, and so forth. I mean they arrive and say, like I am Truman Capote. Well, they look a bit like him so you are taken in by the announcement, I am Truman Capote and you receive him cordially only to find out later it isn't the true Truman Capote it's the false Truman Capote. Last summer I had the false Truman Capote and the year before that I had the false Mary McCarthy. That's before I took to checking the passports of sudden visitors. Well, – [*She crosses to the other chair and sits opposite him.*] – as far as I know they're still down there in that little grass hut on the beach where undesirables are transferred to when the villas are overcrowded. The Oubliette. A medieval institution that I think personally was discarded too soon. It was a dungeon, where people were put for keeps to be forgotten. You say you know about it?

[CHRIS *stares straight at her, not answering by word or gesture: his look is gentle, troubled.*]

So that's what I call my little grass shack on the beach, I call it the oubliette from the French verb 'oublier' which means to forget, to forget, to put away and –

CHRIS: – forget . . .

MRS GOFORTH: And I do really forget 'em. Maybe you think I'm joking but it's the truth. Can't stand to be made a Patsy. Understand what I mean?

[*He nods.*]

This is nothing personal. You came with your book – [*She picks up his book of poetry.*] – with a photograph of you on it which still looks like you just, well, ten years younger, but still unmistakably you. You're not the false Chris Flanders, I'm sure about that.

CHRIS: Thank you. I try not to be.

MRS GOFORTH: However, I don't keep up with the new personalities in the world of art like I used to. Too much a waste of vital energy, Chris. Of course you're not exactly a new personality in it: would you say so?

[CHRIS *smiles: shakes his head slightly.*]

You're almost a veteran in it. I said a veteran, I didn't say a 'has been' – [*She sneezes violently.*] I'm allergic to something around here. I haven't found out just what, but when I do, oh, brother, watch it go!

CHRIS [*who has risen and brought her a clean tissue*]: I hope it isn't the bougainvillaea vines.

MRS GOFORTH: No, it isn't the bougainvillaea, but I'm having an allergy specialist flown down here from Rome to check me with every goddam plant and animal on the place, and whatever it is has to go.

CHRIS: Have you tried breathing sea water?

MRS GOFORTH: Oh, you want to drown me?

CHRIS [*crossing back to his chair and sitting*]: Ha ha, no, I meant have you tried snuffing it up your nostrils to irrigate your nasal passages, Mrs Goforth, it's sometimes a very effective treatment for –

MRS GOFORTH: Aside from this allergy and a little neuralgia, sometimes more than a little, I'm a healthy woman. Know how I've kept in shape, my body the way it still is?

CHRIS: – Exercise?

MRS GOFORTH: Yes! In bed! Plenty of it, still going on! . . . but there's this worship of youth in the States, this Whistler's Mother complex, you know what I mean, this idea that at a certain age a woman ought to resign herself to being a sweet old thing in a rocker. Well, last weekend, a man, a *young* man, came in my bedroom and it wasn't too easy to get him out of it. I had to be very firm about it.

[BLACKIE *appears on the terrace with a plate of food for* CHRIS – MRS GOFORTH *rises.*]

– What've you got there, Blackie?

BLACKIE: Mr Flanders' breakfast, I'm sure he would like some.

MRS GOFORTH: Aw, now, isn't that thoughtful. Put it down there.

[*As* BLACKIE *starts to put it down on the table,* MRS GOFORTH *indicates the serving table.*]

I said down there, and get me my menthol inhaler and Kleenex. I have run out.

[BLACKIE *sets the plate on the serving table and retires from the lighted area.*]

Simonetta!

[MRS GOFORTH *rings and hands the tray to* SIMONETTA *who has entered.*]

Take this away. I can't stand the smell of food now.

[SIMONETTA *exits.*]

CHRIS [*who has moved toward the serving table, stands stunned*]: Mrs Goforth, I feel that I have, I must have disturbed you, annoyed you – disturbed you because I – [*He crosses back to the table.*]

MRS GOFORTH: Don't reach for a cigarette till I offer you one.

CHRIS: May I have one, Mrs Goforth?

MRS GOFORTH: Take one. Be my Trojan Horse Guest. Wait.

[*She moves down beside him.*] Kiss me for it.

[CHRIS *doesn't move.*]

Kiss me for it, I told you.

CHRIS [*putting the cigarette away*]: Mrs Goforth, there are moments for kisses and moments not for kisses.

MRS GOFORTH: This is a 'not for kiss' moment?

[*He turns away and she follows and takes his arm.*]

I've shocked *you* by my ferocity, have I? Sometimes I shock myself by it.

[*They move together towards the balustrade.*]

Look: a coin has two sides. On one side is an eagle but on the other side is – something else . . .

CHRIS: Yes, something else: usually some elderly potentate's profile.

[*She laughs appreciatively at his* riposte . . . *touches his shoulder: he moves a step away from her.*]

MRS GOFORTH: Why didn't you grab the plate and run off with it?

CHRIS: Like a dog grabs a bone?

MRS GOFORTH: Sure! Why not? It might've pleased me to see you show some fight.

CHRIS: I can fight if I have to, but the fighting style of dogs is not my style.

MRS GOFORTH: *Grab, fight, or go hungry!* – nothing else works.

CHRIS: How is it possible for a woman of your reputation as a patron of arts and artists, to live up here, with all this beauty about you, and yet be –

MRS GOFORTH: A bitch, a swamp-bitch, a devil? Oh, I see it, the view, but it makes me feel ugly this summer for some reason or other: – bitchy, a female devil.

CHRIS: You'd like the view to be ugly to make you superior to it?

MRS GOFORTH [*turning to him*]: Why don't we sing that old church hymn,

> 'From Greenland's icy mountains to India's coral isle
> Everything is beautiful' . . .

CHRIS: 'Man alone is vile.'

MRS GOFORTH: – Hmm. – Devils can be driven out of the heart by the touch of a hand on a hand or a mouth on a mouth. Because, like Alex said once, 'Evil isn't a person: evil is a thing that comes sneaky-snaking into the heart of a person, and takes it over: a mean intruder, a *squatter!*'

CHRIS [*crossing to her*]: May I touch your hand, please?

MRS GOFORTH [*as he does*]: Your hand's turned cold, I've shocked the warm blood out of it. Let me rub it back in.

CHRIS: Your hand's cold, too, Mrs Goforth.

MRS GOFORTH: Oh, that's just – nervous tension, never mind that. – I'll tell you something, Chris, you came here at a time unusually favourable to you. Now we're going to talk turkey, at least, I'm going to talk turkey, you can talk ducks and geese but I am going to talk turkey, cold turkey. You've come here at a time when I'm restless, bored and shocked by the news of deaths of three friends in the States, one, two, three, like fire-crackers going off, right together almost, like rat-a-tat-tat blindfolded against the wall. – Well, you see I – [*She moves down to the lower terrace.*] – I had a bad scare last winter. I was visiting relatives I'd set up on a grand estate on Long Island when some little psychosomatic symptom gave me a scare. They made a big deal of it, had me removed by a seaplane to the East River where they had an ambulance waiting for me, and whisked me off to a – Know what I said when I was advised to go under the knife the next day? Ha, I'll tell you, ha ha! – Called my law firm and dictated a letter cutting them off with one dollar apiece in my will . . .

CHRIS [*who has come down to her*]: Mrs Goforth, are you still afraid of – [*He hesitates.*]

MRS GOFORTH: Death – never even think of it.

[*She takes his arm and they move down to a bench and sit.*]

CHRIS: Death is one moment and life is so many of them.

MRS GOFORTH: A million billion of them if you think in terms of a lifetime as rich as mine's been, Chris.

CHRIS: Yes, life is something, death's nothing . . .

MRS GOFORTH: Nothing, nothing, but nothing – I've had to refer to many deaths in my memoirs, – Oh, I don't think I'm immortal. I still go to sleep every night wondering if I'll – wake up the next day . . . [*Coughs: gasps for breath.*] – face that angry old lion.

CHRIS: Angry old –?

MRS GOFORTH: – Lion!

CHRIS: The sun? You think it's angry?

MRS GOFORTH: Naturally, of course; looking down on –? – well, you know what it looks down on . . .

CHRIS: It seems to accept and understand things today . . .

MRS GOFORTH: It's just a big fire-ball that toughens the skin, including the skin of the heart.

CHRIS: – How lovely the evenings must be here – when the fishing boats go out on the Gulf of Salerno with their little lamps shining.

MRS GOFORTH: Well, they call this coast the *Divina Costiera*, that means the divine coast, you know.

CHRIS: Yes, I know – I suppose . . .

MRS GOFORTH: You suppose what?

CHRIS: I suppose you dine on the terrace about the time the fishing boats go out with their little lamps and the stars come out of the –

MRS GOFORTH: Firmament, call it the firmament, not the sky, it's much more classy to call it the firmament, baby. How about spring? You write about spring and live in it, you write about love in the spring, haven't you written love-poems for susceptible – patrons? – Well! How many books of poems have you come out with?

CHRIS: Just the one that I brought you.

MRS GOFORTH: You mean you burnt out as a poet?

CHRIS: – Pardon?

MRS GOFORTH: You mean you burnt out as a poet?

[CHRIS *laughs uncomfortably.*]

Why're you laughing? I didn't say anything funny.

CHRIS: I didn't know I was laughing. Excuse me, Mrs Goforth. But you are very – direct.

MRS GOFORTH: Is that shocking?

CHRIS: No. – No, not really. In fact I like that about you.

MRS GOFORTH: Each time you give that little embarrassed laugh like I'd made you uncomfortable.

CHRIS: My nerves are –

MRS GOFORTH: Gone through like your list of suckers.

[MRS GOFORTH *sneezes and crosses away for another tissue.*]

CHRIS [*standing*]: Mrs Goforth – if you want me to go –

MRS GOFORTH: That depends.

CHRIS: – What does it depend on?

MRS GOFORTH: – Frankly, I'm very lonely up here this summer.

CHRIS: – I can understand that.

MRS GOFORTH: Now you're not stupid. You're attractive to me. You know that you are. You've deliberately set out to be attractive to me and you are. So don't be a free-loader.

[*Pause.*]

CHRIS: Mrs Goforth, I think you've been exposed to the wrong kind of people and –

MRS GOFORTH [*cutting in*]: I'm sick of moral blackmail! You know what that is. People imposing on you by the old, old trick of making you feel it would be unkind of you not to permit them to do it. In their hearts they despise you. So much they can't quite hide it. It pops out in sudden little remarks and looks they give you. Busting with malice – Because you have what they haven't. You know what some writer called it? 'A robust conscience, and the Viking spirit in life!'

CHRIS [*crossing back on terrace*]: Oh? Is that what he called it?

MRS GOFORTH [*following*]: He called it that, and I have it! I give away nothing, I sell and I buy in my life, and I've always wound up with a profit, one way or another. You came up that hill from the highway with an old book of poems that you got published ten years ago, by playing on the terrible, desperate loneliness of a rich old broken-hipped woman, who, all she could do, was pretend that someone still loved her.

CHRIS: You're talking about Mrs Ferguson.

MRS GOFORTH: Yes, I am.

CHRIS [*moving up away from her*]: I made her walk again. She published my poems.

MRS GOFORTH: How long after she published your poems did you let go of her arm so she fell on the deck of a steamship and her hip broke again?

CHRIS: – I didn't let her go. She broke away from me,

[MRS GOFORTH *laughs uproariously.*]

if you'll allow me to make a minor correction in the story. We were walking very slowly about the promenade deck of the *Queen Mary*, eight summers ago, more than a year after my poems were published. A young man called to her from a deck-chair that we'd just passed, and she wheeled around and broke away from my hand, and slipped and fell and her hip was broken again. Of course some malicious 'friends' blamed me, but – I wouldn't leave her.

MRS GOFORTH: No? She was still your meal-ticket?

CHRIS: Not at all.

MRS GOFORTH: Who *was*?

CHRIS [*sitting*]: – I was fashionable, then.

MRS GOFORTH: Do you sit down while a lady is standing?

CHRIS [*springs up with a rather ferocious smile*]: Sorry, won't you sit down!

[*His tone is so commanding, abruptly, that she does sit down in the chair he jerks out for her.*]

– May I tell you something about yourself? It may seem presumptuous of me to tell you this but I'm going to tell you this: you're suffering more than you need to.

MRS GOFORTH: I am –

CHRIS [*cutting through her protest*]: You're suffering from the worst of all human maladies, all afflictions, and I don't mean one of the body, I mean the thing people feel when they go from room to room for no reason, and then they go back from room to room for no reason, and then they go *out* for no reason and come back *in* for no reason –

MRS GOFORTH: You mean I'm alone here, don't you?

[CHRIS *takes hold of her hand.*]

MRS GOFORTH [*snatching her hand away from him*]: I'm WORKING up here this summer, WORKING! EVER HEARD OF IT?

[*A* STAGE ASSISTANT *appears in the wings as if she had shouted for him. He hands her a letter.*]

This morning's mail brought me this! My London publisher's letter! 'Darling Flora: Your book of memoirs, *Facts and a Figure* – will, in my opinion, rank with and possibly –

[*Squints in the glare, unable to decipher the letter further.*
He removes it from her trembling, jewelled hand, and completes the reading.]

CHRIS: '– rank with and possibly even out-rank the great Marcel Proust's *Remembrance of Things Past* as a social documentation of two continents in three decades . . .'

MRS GOFORTH: *Well?*

CHRIS: A letter like this should fall on a higher mountain.

MRS GOFORTH: Huh?

CHRIS: A letter like this should be delivered above the snow-line of an Alpine peak because it's snow, a snow-job.

[*She snatches it back from him.*]

MRS GOFORTH [*raging*]: For you, a blond beatnik, coming from Naples on foot up a goddam goat-path, wearing at this table a Japanese robe because dogs tore your britches, I think your presumption is not excusable, Mister. It lacks the excuse of much youth, you're not young enough for your moxey. This publisher's not a lover, a lover might snow me but this man's a business associate and they don't snow you, not ME, not SISSY GOFORTH!

They don't snow me – SNOW me! They don't get up that early in the morning –

[*Her agitation somehow touches him: His smile turns warm again.*]

– that they could – [*laughs.*] – snow me . . .

[*The* STAGE ASSISTANTS *lean whispering together as they retire from the stage.*]

CHRIS: Of course without having your publisher's advantage of knowing *Facts and a Figure* –

MRS GOFORTH: Nothing, not a word of it!

CHRIS: No, not a word, but what I was going to say was that I think you need *companionship*: not just employees about you, up here, but – how often do you see old friends or new friends this summer, Mrs Goforth? Often or not so often?

MRS GOFORTH: Hell, all I have to do is pick up a phone to crowd this mountain with –

CHRIS: CROWDS: Is it that easy this summer? You're proud. You don't want to ask people up here that might not come, because they're pleasure-seekers, frantic choosers of silly little distractions, and – and –

MRS GOFORTH: 'and and' WHAT?

CHRIS: Your condition, the terrible strain of your work, makes you seem – eccentric, disturbing! – To those sea-level, those lower than sea-level people . . .

MRS GOFORTH: GET TO WHATEVER YOU'RE LEADING UP TO, WILL YOU!

CHRIS: I notice you have trouble reading. I've been told I have a good reading voice.

MRS GOFORTH: Most human voices are very monotonous to me. Besides, I'm more interested in producing literature this summer than having it read to me.

CHRIS: Mmm, but you do need some agreeable companionship.

MRS GOFORTH: Right you are about *that*, but how do I know your idea of agreeable companionship is the same as mine? You purr at me like a cat, now, but a cat will purr at you one minute and scratch your eyes out the next.

[*He leans back, smiling, working the sword up and down in its scabbard.*]

I think you'd better take off that old sword-belt.

CHRIS: There's no buttons on the robe so without the belt on it –

MRS GOFORTH: Take it off you!

CHRIS: The *robe*?

MRS GOFORTH: The *sword*-belt. You grin and fiddle with the hilt – the sword like you had – evil – intentions.

CHRIS: Oh. You suspect I'm a possible assassin?

MRS GOFORTH: *Take it off, give it here!*

CHRIS: All right: formal surrender, *unconditional . . . nearly.*

[*Takes the sword-belt off and hands it to her.*]

MRS GOFORTH: *OK. Robert E. Lee!: At Appomatox . . .*

[*Hurls the sword-belt to the terrace tiles behind her.*]
[*A* STAGE ASSISTANT *darts out of the wings to remove it: the other* ASSISTANT *laughs offstage.*]

CHRIS: Now what can I use for a sash to keep things proper?

MRS GOFORTH: See if this goes around you, if being proper's so important to you. [*Hands him a brilliant scarf she wore about her throat.*]

[*He turns upstage to tie the scarf about him.*
A phone is heard ringing, off.
BLACKIE *appears from behind the library screen.*]

MRS GOFORTH: Who's calling, my broker again, with the closing quotations?

BLACKIE: The call's for *Mr Flanders*.

CHRIS: *Me*, for *me*? But who could know I'm up here!

MRS GOFORTH: Cut the bull, you got a call up here last night; business is picking up for you.

CHRIS: This is – mystifying!

BLACKIE: The phone's in the library.

CHRIS: Excuse me. [*Crosses quickly behind the library screen.*]

[MRS GOFORTH *crosses toward it but remains, listening, outside it.*]

CHRIS'S VOICE [*behind screen*]: *Pronto, sono pronto. – Madelyn!* – How are you, how's your dear mother? – Oh, my God! – I meant to come straight down there but – was it, uh, what they call *peaceful*? Oh, I'm so glad, I prayed so hard that it *would* be! And I'm so relieved that it *was*. I did so long to be with you but had to stop on the way. And you? Will you be all right? – Yes, I know, expected, but still I could be some use in making the necessary arrangements? I'm at Flora Goforth's place, but if you could send a car to pick me up I could – Oh? – Well, Madelyn, all I can say is *accept* it. – Bless you, goodbye: *accept* it.

[MRS GOFORTH *is shaken: she moves back to the table as if she had received a personal shock.*

CHRIS *comes back out: at the same moment, church-bells ring in a village below the mountain.*]

CHRIS: – Church-bells? In the village?

MRS GOFORTH: Yes, appropriate, aren't they? Ringing right on a dead cue . . .

CHRIS: – I just received news that's – *shocked* me . . .

MRS GOFORTH: Another name you have to scratch off the list?

CHRIS: – Did you say 'list'?

[MRS GOFORTH *smiles at him cunningly, fiercely.*]

MRS GOFORTH: – I went to a spiritualist once. She said to me, 'I hear many dead voices calling, Flora, Flora.' I knew she was a fake, then, since all my close friends call me Sissy. I said, 'Tell them to mind their own business, play their gold harps and mind their own harp-playing, Sissy Goforth's not ready to go forth yet and won't go forth till she's ready . . .'

[*The bell stops ringing.*
CHRIS *extends a hand to her.*]

MRS GOFORTH: What are you reaching out for?

CHRIS: Your hand, if I may, Mrs Goforth. [*He has taken hold of it.*]

MRS GOFORTH: Hold it but don't squeeze it, the rings cut my fingers.

CHRIS: I'm glad we've talked so frankly, so quickly today. The conversation we had at the ball at the Waldorf in 1950 was a long conversation but not as deep as this one.

MRS GOFORTH: Who said anything deep? I don't say anything deep in a conversation, not this summer, I save it for my memoirs. Did you say anything deep, in your opinion? If you did, it escaped me, escaped my notice completely. Oh, you've known Swanees. Excuse me: Swamis. You've been exposed to the – the intellectual scene and it's rubbed off on you a little, but only skin-deep, as deep as your little blond beard . . .

CHRIS: Perhaps I used the wrong word.

[*She places a cigarette in her mouth and waits for him to light it. He turns deliberately away from her and places a foot on the low balustrade, facing seaward.*]

– This 'wine-dark sea', it's the oldest sea in the world . . .

MRS GOFORTH: What deep remark was that?

CHRIS: Only the sea down there has said anything deep: *boom!* – that's deep. Looking down there, do you know what I see?

MRS GOFORTH: The sea.

CHRIS: Yes, and a fleet of Roman triremes, those galleys with three banks of oars, rowed by slaves, commanded by commanders headed for conquests. Out for loot. *Boom!* Out for conquering, pillaging and collecting more slaves. *Boom!* Here's where the whole show started, it's the oldest sea in the Western world, Mrs Goforth, this sea called the Mediterranean Sea, which means the middle of earth, was the cradle of life, not the grave but the cradle of pagan and Christian – civilizations, this sea, and its connecting river, that old water-snake, the Nile.

MRS GOFORTH: I've been on the Nile. No message. Couple of winters ago I stayed at the Mena House, that hotel under the pyramids. I could see the pyramids, those big – big calcified fools-caps from my breakfast balcony. No message. Rode up to 'em on a camel so I could say I'd done the whole bit.

CHRIS: No message?

MRS GOFORTH: No message except you can get seasick on a camel, yep, you can get mighty seasick on the hump of a camel. Went inside those old king-size tombstones.

CHRIS: No message inside them, either?

MRS GOFORTH: No message except the Pharaohs and families had the idiotic idea they were going to wake up hungry and thirsty and had provided themselves with breakfasts which had gone very stale and dry and the Pharaohs and families were still sound asleep, ho ho . . .

[*He still has his back to her: she is obviously annoyed by his lost attention to her.*]

And if you look this way you'll notice I've got a cigarette in my mouth and I'm waiting for you to light it. Didn't that old Sally Ferguson bitch teach you to light a cigarette for a lady?

CHRIS [*facing her*]: She wasn't a bitch unless all old dying ladies are bitches. She was dying, and scared to death of dying, which made her a little – eccentric . . .

[*He has picked up* MRS GOFORTH's *diamond-studded lighter. He lights her cigarette but doesn't return the lighter to the table: tosses it in the palm of his hand.*]

MRS GOFORTH: Thanks. Now put it down.

[*He sits down, smiling, on the low balustrade: there has been a marked change in his surface attitude toward her: the deferential air has gone completely.*]

I meant my Bulgari lighter, not your – *backside*!

[*He studies the lighter as if to calculate its value. Pause.*]

– If you don't put that lighter back down on the table I'm going to call for Rudy! You know Rudy, you've made his acquaintance, I think.

CHRIS: If I don't put it down on the table but in my pocket and if I ran down the goat-path with it – how fast can Rudy run?

MRS GOFORTH: How fast can *you* run? Could you out-run the dogs? Yesterday you didn't out-run the dogs.

CHRIS: That was – up-hill, on the other side of your mountain. I think I could get down this side, yes, by the – funicular, I could operate it.

MRS GOFORTH: Can you out-run a bullet?

CHRIS: Oh, would you have Rudy shoot at me for this lighter?

MRS GOFORTH: You bet I would. That's a very valuable lighter.

[CHRIS *laughs and tosses the lighter on the table.*]

CHRIS: – Hmmm. – On a parapet over the Western world's oldest sea, the lady that owns it had a gangster –

MRS GOFORTH: The bodyguard of a syndicate gangster!

CHRIS: Yes, the lady that owns it had her bodyguard shoot down a – what? – burnt-out poet who had confiscated a diamond-studded lighter because he was unfed and hungry, he'd been on a five-day fast for – non-secular reasons and it had upset his reason.

[MRS GOFORTH *rings the bell on the table.*
CHRIS *seizes her hand and wrests the bell away from it.*
She rises from the table and shouts: 'RUDY!']

CHRIS [louder]: *RUDY!*

MRS GOFORTH: You couldn't get away with it!

CHRIS: Oh, yes, I could: if I wanted. [*He tosses the lighter back on the table with a mocking grin.*]

MRS GOFORTH: What a peculiar – puzzlesome young man you are! You came out here like a dandy, kissed my hand, and now you're coming on like a young hood all of a sudden, and I don't like the change, it makes me nervous with you, and now I don't know if I want you around here or not, or if I'm – not superstitious. See? You've made me shaky.

CHRIS: You didn't know I was teasing?

MRS GOFORTH: No. You're too good at it.

CHRIS [*turning seaward again*]: I see it, your oubliette on the beach, it looks attractive to me.

MRS GOFORTH: – Help me into my bedroom. [*Tries to rise: falls back into the chair.*] – It's time for my siesta.

CHRIS: Could I stay there, a while?

MRS GOFORTH: Later maybe: now now: I need to rest.

CHRIS: I meant the grass hut on the beach, not your bedroom.

MRS GOFORTH: Be still, she's coming back out, my secretary, and I'm not sure I trust her.

CHRIS: Do you trust anybody?

MRS GOFORTH: Nobody human, just dogs. All except poodles, I never trusted a poodle . . .

[BLACKIE *comes on to the terrace.*]

In again, out again, Finnegan! What's it *this* time, Blackie?

BLACKIE: Is it true you've discharged the kitchen staff, Mrs Goforth?

MRS GOFORTH: Yes, it's true . . . Haven't you heard about the inventory?

BLACKIE: What inventory, inventory of what?

MRS GOFORTH: I had an intuition that things were disappearing and had Rudy check my list of fabulous china, my Sèvres, Limoges, Lowenstoff, against what was still on the mountain. Half of it gone, decimated! And my Medici silver, banquet silver used by the Medicis hundreds of years ago, GONE! – That's what the inventory disclosed!

BLACKIE: Mrs Goforth, is it possible you don't remember –

MRS GOFORTH: WHAT?

BLACKIE: You had it removed to a storage house in Naples, in an armoured truck.

MRS GOFORTH: ME?

BLACKIE: YOU!

MRS GOFORTH: NOT TRUE!

BLACKIE: Mrs Goforth, when people are very ill and taking drugs for it, they get confused, their memories are confused, they get delusions.

MRS GOFORTH: THIS MOUNTAIN HAS BEEN SYSTEMATICALLY PILLAGED! – That's what the inventory –

BLACKIE: An inventory made by the bodyguard of a syndicate gangster?

MRS GOFORTH: *How dare you suggest – I have a guest at the table!*

BLACKIE: *I will always dare to say what I know to be true!*

MRS GOFORTH: *Go in, find my cheque-book and write out a cheque for yourself for whatever's coming to you, and bring it out here and I'll sign*

it for cash, at the Naples branch of my bank! You wanted out, now you
got it, so TAKE IT! TAKE IT!

BLACKIE: *Gladly! Gladly!*

MRS GOFORTH: Mutually *gladly! GO IN!*

> [BLACKIE *starts off:* MRS GOFORTH's *shouting has brought on a
> coughing spasm. She covers her mouth with her hands and rushes, in
> a crouched position, toward the upstage area of the library.*]

CHRIS: – *Boom* . . .

BLACKIE: *Release!*

CHRIS: Blackie? Look! – [*Points at the terrace pavement.*] – Blood, she's
bleeding . . .

MRS GOFORTH'S VOICE [*offstage, hoarsely*]: DOTTORE CHIAME
LO DOTTORE! GIULIO, SIMONETTA!

CHRIS: You'd better go in there with her.

BLACKIE: I can't yet. They'll get the doctor for her. [*She moves downstage, gasping.*] You see, she's made me *inhuman!*

> [GIULIO *and* SIMONETTA *explode on to the forestage.*]

SIMONETTA: *Signorina, la Signora e molto, molto malatta!*

BLACKIE [*crossing to her*]: Dov'è la Signora, in camera da letto?

SIMONETTA: *No, nella libreria, con il dottore!* [*She sits on a bench and sobs
hysterically.*]

BLACKIE: Well, I'd better go in there.

CHRIS: What shall I do? Anything?

BLACKIE: Yes, stay here, don't go.

> [*Then to* SIMONETTA *who is now crying theatrically.*]

Ferma questa – commedia.

> [SIMONETTA *stops and begins straightening up the table. To* CHRIS]

Call the hospital in Rome, Salvatore Mundi, and ask for Dr Rengucci. Tell him what's happening here and a nurse is needed at
once. Then come in there, the library, and we'll –

> [GIULIO *rushes out.*]

GIULIO: Signora Goforth vuol vedere il Signore, presto, molto presto!

BLACKIE: She's calling for *you*. – I'd better go in first. Make the call and then come to the library.

[*She exits one way:* CHRIS *the other.*]

GIULIO [*To* SIMONETTA]: She's dying?

SIMONETTA: No one's paid this week, who will pay us if she dies today?

GIULIO: *Guarda!* [*He displays a gold bracelet.*]

[SIMONETTA *snatches at it.* GIULIO *pockets it with a grin and starts off as she follows.*]

SCENE DIMS OUT

Scene Six

A while later, toward sundown. The interiors of the white villa are screened and the terrace is lighted more coolly.

BLACKIE is seated at the downstage table, jotting memoranda in a notebook, of things to be done before leaving.

The STAGE ASSISTANTS stand by the flag-staff ready to lower the banner of MRS GOFORTH.

ONE: Cable her daughter that the old bitch is dying.

TWO: The banner of the Griffin is about to be lowered.

BLACKIE [*as if translating their speech into a polite paraphrase*]: Cable Mrs Goforth's daughter at Point Goforth, Long Island, that her mother is not expected to survive the night: and I'm waiting for – immediate – instructions.

ONE: Fireworks tonight at Point Goforth, Long Island.

TWO: A champagne fountain.

TOGETHER: Death: Celebration.

BLACKIE: Call police in Amalfi to guard the library safe till Rudy has gone.

ONE: Rudy's root-a-toot-tooting through that safe right now.

TWO: He's disappointed to discover that the old bitch still has on her most important jewels.

ONE: And she's still conscious; fiercely.

BLACKIE: Contact mortuary. Amalfi.

TWO: That Blackie's a cool one.

[CHRIS *comes on to the terrace, now wearing his repaired* lederhosen *and a washed but unironed white shirt.*]

137

CHRIS: Blackie?

BLACKIE [*glancing up*]: Oh. I'm making out a list of things to do before leaving.

CHRIS: You're not leaving right away, are you?

BLACKIE: Soon as I get instructions from her daughter.

CHRIS: I called the Rome doctor and told him what had happened. He said he's expected it sooner and there's nothing more to be done that can't be done by the doctor on the place.

BLACKIE: The little doctor, Lullo, has given her a strong shot of adrenalin which was a mistake, I think. She won't go to bed, keeps pressing electric buzzers for Simonetta who's run away, and she's put on all her rings so they won't be stolen: she's more afraid of being robbed of her jewellery than her life. What time would it be in the States?

CHRIS: What time is it here?

BLACKIE: Sundown, nearly.

CHRIS: About seven-thirty here would make it – about two-thirty there.

BLACKIE: Maybe a phone-call would get through before a cable.

[*Rises; one of the* STAGE ASSISTANTS *brings a phone from the table by the chaise-longue, a little upstage.*
Taking the phone.]

Try her daughter's husband at *Goforth, Faller and Rush, Incorporated*, Plaza 1–9000, while I – [*She gives* CHRIS *the phone and pours herself a brandy.*]

[RUDY *comes out with a strong box from the safe.*]

BLACKIE: Who's that? Oh! YOU! What are you taking out?

RUDY: Just what I was told to take out.

BLACKIE: Well, take it out, but don't forget that everything's been listed.

RUDY: I don't forget nothing, Blackie. [*Goes off.*]

STAGE ASSISTANT ONE [*removing the crested screen*]: Her bedroom in the white villa.

TWO: The griffin is staring at death, and trying to out-stare it.

[*We see* MRS GOFORTH *seated: she wears a majestic ermine-trimmed robe to which she has pinned her 'most important jewels', and rings blaze on her fingers that clench the chair-arms.*]

ONE: Her eyes are bright as her diamonds.

TWO: Until she starts bleeding again, she'll give no ground to any real or suspected adversary . . .

ONE: And *then*?

[*During this exchange between the* ASSISTANTS, *who back into the wings, now, on their soundless shoes,* BLACKIE *has made several other notations: now, without looking up at* CHRIS, *she asks him –*]

BLACKIE: You're still very hungry, aren't you?

CHRIS: Yes, very.

BLACKIE: The new kitchen staff has arrived. I've put a bottle of milk in your rucksack and your rucksack is in the library. You'd better just have the milk now: we'll have dinner later together.

CHRIS: Blackie, I've seen her grass hut on the beach, her oubliette, as she calls it. And –

BLACKIE: (?)

CHRIS: I wonder how long I could stay down there before I'd be discovered and – evicted?

BLACKIE: Long as you want to, indefinitely, I guess, but how would you live down there with the villas all closed?

CHRIS: On, on – *frutta de mare:* shell-fish. – And I'd make a spear for spear-fishing.

BLACKIE: There's no fresh water down there, just the sea water.

CHRIS: I know how to make fresh water out of sea-water.

BLACKIE: Why would you want to stay down there?

CHRIS [*as a wave crashes under the mountain*]: BOOM! I'd like to make a mobile; I'd call it BOOM. The sea and the sky are turning the same colour, dissolving into each other. Wine-dark sea and wine-dark sky. In a little while the little fishing boats with their lamps for night fishing will make the sea look like the night sky turned upside down, and you and I will have a sort of valedictory dinner on the terrace.

BLACKIE: Yes, it sounds very peaceful . . .

[*The bedroom of the white villa is brightened:* MRS GOFORTH *staggers from her chair, knocking it over. The* STAGE ASSISTANTS *dart out to snatch the small chair up and move it further upstage, as she leans on a bed-post, gasping. Then she draws herself up: advances to the chair's new position a little further upstage. She reaches out for it. The* ASSISTANTS *draw it further upstage. She staggers dizzily after it. The* ASSISTANTS *exchange inquiring looks at each other: silently agree to allow her the chair: back out of the area. She sits down with a cry of fury and resumes her fierce contest with death: a reserve of power, triggered by the adrenalin, begins to re-animate her: she rises and drags the chair to a small boudoir table and calls out –.*]

MRS GOFORTH: CHRIS? CHRIS?

BLACKIE: That's her, she's calling for you. – Can you stand to go in there?

CHRIS: Sure I can – It's a professional duty.

[*As he turns upstage the* STAGE ASSISTANTS *remove the screen masking the library: he enters that area: one of the* STAGE ASSISTANTS *turns the screen perpendicular to the proscenium so that it represents a wall-division between bedroom and library.*]

BOOM!

Mrs Goforth?

MRS GOFORTH: Oh, you've finally got here. Stay out there, don't come in here right away. The doctor gave me a shot that's made me a little dizzy, I'll call you in – in a minute . . .

[*She staggers up from the chair, knocking it over.*]

CHRIS: – Are you all right, Mrs Goforth? [*He discovers his sack: removes and opens the milk bottle.*]

MRS GOFORTH: Just a little unsteady after the shot, the doctor said. The bleeding was from a little blood-vessel at the back of my throat. But he thinks I ought to lay off the work for a while, just wind up this volume and save the rest for – sequels . . .

[CHRIS *opens the milk bottle and sips the milk as if it were sacramental wine.*]

– Don't you think that's better, since it's such a strain on me?

CHRIS: Yes, I do, I think it's a – [*Drinks milk.*] – a wise decision . . . [*He catches some drops of milk that have run down his chin: licks them almost reverently off the palm of his hand.*]

[MRS GOFORTH *enters the library.*]

MRS GOFORTH: All that work, the pressure, was burning me up, it was literally burning me up like a house on fire.

[*He assists her to the desk chair.*]

CHRIS: Yes, we – all live in a house on fire, no fire-department to call; no way out, just the upstairs windows to look out of while the fire burns the house down with us trapped, locked in it.

MRS GOFORTH: What do you mean by – what windows?

CHRIS [*touching his forehead*]: These upstairs windows, not wide enough to crawl out of, just wide enough to lean out of and look out of, and – look and look and look, till we're almost nothing but looking, nothing, almost, but *vision* . . .

MRS GOFORTH: Hmmm. – Yes. – It isn't as cool out here as it was in my bedroom and this robe I've put on is too heavy. So come on in. We can talk in my bedroom. [*She retires behind bedroom screen.*]

MRS GOFORTH'S VOICE [*from behind her screen*]: Talking between rooms is a strain on the ears and the vocal cords – so come in, now: I'm ready.

[*He crosses to the screens: stops short.*]

CHRIS: Oh. Sorry. [*He turns away from the screens.*] I'll wait till you've –

MRS GOFORTH'S VOICE: Modesty? *Modesty?* I wouldn't expect you to suffer from modesty, Chris. I never was bothered with silliness of that kind. If you've got a figure that's pleasing to look at, why be selfish with it?

CHRIS: Yes, it *was* a pleasure, Mrs Goforth.

MRS GOFORTH'S VOICE: Then why'd you retreat, back away? In my bedroom, in here, I almost never, if ever, wear a stitch of clothes, in summer. I like to feel cool air on my bare skin in summer. Don't you like that? Cool air and cool water on the bare skin in summer's the nicest thing about summer. Huh? Don't you think so, too?

CHRIS: I've found my duffle-bag. It wandered in here, for some reason.

MRS GOFORTH'S VOICE: I had it brought there so I could get your passport for the local police. They want a look at the passport of anyone just arrived.

CHRIS: I see.

MRS GOFORTH'S VOICE: You'll get it back when you go, you know, there's no hurry, is there?

CHRIS: I'm not sure about that. [*Finds passport.*] Anyway, it's already been returned.

MRS GOFORTH: We've just been getting acquainted. The preliminaries of a friendship, or any kind of relationship, are the most difficult part, and our talk on the terrace was just a – *preliminary*.

CHRIS [*wryly, beneath her hearing*]: Sometimes the preliminaries are rougher than the main bout. [*He is rearranging the articles in the rucksack.*]

MRS GOFORTH: I didn't catch that. What was that?

CHRIS [*to himself*]: I didn't mean you to catch it.

MRS GOFORTH: Stop mumbling and fussing with that metal stuff in the sack, the fussing drowns out the mumbling. D'ya want me to break another blood vessel in my throat talking to you from here?

CHRIS: Are you dressed now, Mrs Goforth?

MRS GOFORTH: Hell, I told you I'm never dressed in my bedroom.

CHRIS: You said 'rarely if ever' – not never. [*He sighs and crosses to the door again.*] – You have a beautiful body, Mrs Goforth. It's a privilege to be permitted to admire it. It makes me think of one of those great fountain figures in Scandinavian countries.

MRS GOFORTH: Yeah, well, baby, a fountain figure is a stone figure, and my body isn't a stone figure, although it's been sculpted by several world-famous sculptors, it's still a flesh and blood figure.

And don't think it's been easy to keep it the way it still is. I'm going to lie down and rest now on this cool bed, mmm, these sheets are so cool, come on in. Why are you standing there paralysed in that door?

CHRIS: I'm – silent on a peak in – *Darien* . . . [*Turns away from the door.*] I came here hoping to be your friend, Mrs Goforth, but –

MRS GOFORTH'S VOICE: You said 'but' something, but what?

CHRIS: I wouldn't have come here unless I thought I was able to serve some purpose or other, in return for a temporary refuge, a place to rest and work in, where I could get back that sense of reality I've been losing lately, as I tried to explain on the terrace, but – [*He has removed the large mobile under her desk: he climbs on the desk to attach the mobile to the chandelier above it.*] – You knew I was hungry but it was 'black coffee or else'.

MRS GOFORTH: Is that why you won't come in here?

CHRIS: It would just be embarrassing for us both if I did. [*He jumps off the desk.*]

MRS GOFORTH: *What's that, what're you doing?*

CHRIS: I hung up a gift I brought you, a mobile called 'The Earth is a Wheel in a Great Big Gambling Casino'. And now I think I should leave, I have a long way to go.

MRS GOFORTH: Just a minute. I'm coming back out there to see this mobile of yours. [*She comes from behind the screen, pulling the regal white robe about her.*] Well, where is it?

CHRIS: Right over your head.

[*She looks up, staggering against the desk.*]

MRS GOFORTH: It doesn't move, doesn't go.

CHRIS: It will, when it's caught by the wind.

[*The mobile begins to turn, casting faint flickers of light.*]

There now, the wind's caught it, it's turning. [*He picks up his canvas sack as if preparing to leave.*]

MRS GOFORTH [*picking up the phone, suddenly*]: Kitchen, cucina, cucina! – Cucina? Uno momento! [*She thrusts phone toward CHRIS.*] Tell the cook what you would like for supper.

CHRIS: Anything, Mrs Goforth.

MRS GOFORTH [*into the phone*]: OK – Cucina? Senta – Pranza questa sera. – Pastini in brodo, per commencare. Capish? – SI! – Poi, una grande pesca, si si, una grandissima pescha, anche – carne freddo, si, si, carne freddo – *ROAST BEEF*, BIF, BEEEEEEF! [*Gasps, catches her breath.*] Prosciutto, legume, tutte, tutte legume. Capito? Poi, una insalata verde. No, mista! Insalata mista, MISTA! – they don't know their own language ... – Poi, dulce, zuppe Inglesa, frutta, fromaggio, tutte fromaggio, e vino, vino, bianco e rosa, una bottiglia de Soave e una bottiglia de – [*Gasps for breath again.*] – Valpolicella. – Hanh? – va bene. ... [*Hangs up.*] This new cook sounds like a – Mau-mau ... She'll probably serve us long pig with – shrunk heads on toothpicks stuck in it ... [*Tries to laugh: coughs. Hanging up phone.*] Now, then, you see you're not just going to be fed, you're going to be wined and dined in high style tonight on the terrace. But meanwhile, we're going to enjoy a long siesta together in the cool of my bedroom which is full of historical treasures, including myself! [*She crosses to the bedroom doors, beckons him commandingly.*]

　　[*He doesn't move.*]

　– Well?!

CHRIS: I'm afraid I came here too late to accept these – invitations.

MRS GOFORTH: Who else has invited you somewhere?

CHRIS: I've passed the point where I wait for invitations but I think I'll be welcomed by the elderly spinster lady whose mother died in Taormina today.

MRS GOFORTH: Not if she's heard your nickname. And Sicily's an island. How'll you get there, can you walk on water?

CHRIS: Your discharged secretary gave me a bottle of milk with some ten thousand lire notes attached to it with a – rubber band. So – goodbye, Mrs Goforth. [*He bends to hoist his rucksack over his shoulder.*]

MRS GOFORTH: Mr Flanders, you have the distinction, the dubious distinction, of being the first man that wouldn't come in my bedroom when invited to enter.

CHRIS: I'm sorry.

MRS GOFORTH: Man bring this up road, huh?

CHRIS: No, I –

MRS GOFORTH: What else? Your book of poems, your calling card? Y'must be running short of 'em, here, take it back! [*She hurls it off her desk to his feet.*] I haven't read it but I can imagine the contents. *Facile sentiment!* To be good a poem's got to be tough and to write a good, tough poem you've got to cut your teeth on the marrow-bone of this world: I think you're still cutting your milk teeth, Mr Flanders.

CHRIS: I know you better than you know me. I admire you: admire you so much that I almost like you: *almost*. I think if that old Greek explorer, Pytheas, hadn't beat you to it by centuries, you would've sailed up through the Gates of Hercules to map out the Western world, and you would have sailed up further and mapped it out better than he did, no storm could've driven you back or changed your course, oh, no, you're nobody's fool, but you're a fool, Mrs Goforth, if you don't know that finally, sooner or later, you need somebody or something to mean God to you, even if it's a cow on the streets of Bombay, or carved rock on the Easter Islands or –

MRS GOFORTH: You came here to bring me *God*, did you?

CHRIS: I didn't say God, I said someone or something to –

MRS GOFORTH: I heard what you said, you said *God*, my eyes are out of focus but not my ears! Well, *bring* Him, I'm ready to lay out a red carpet for him, but how do you bring Him? Whistle? Ring a bell for Him? [*She snatches a bell off her desk and rings it fiercely.*] HUH? HOW? WHAT? [*She staggers back against the desk, gasping.*]

CHRIS: I've failed, I've disappointed some people in what they wanted or thought they wanted from me, Mrs Goforth, but sometimes, once in a while, I've given them what they needed even if they didn't know what it was. I brought it up the road to them, and that's how I got the name that's made me unwelcome this summer.

STAGE ASSISTANT: Tell her about the first time!

TOGETHER: Tell her, tell her, the first time!

[*They draw back to the wings.*

The HARMONIUM PLAYER *begins to play softly.*]

CHRIS: – I was at Mrs Ferguson's mountain over Palm Springs, the first time. I wasn't used to her world of elegant bitches and dandies ... Early one morning I went down the mountain and across the desert on a walking trip to a village in Baja, California, where a great Hindu teacher had gathered a group of pupils, disciples, about him. Along the road I passed a rest-home that looked like a grand hotel, and just a little further along, I came to an inlet, an estuary of the ocean, and I stopped for a swim off the beach that was completely deserted, swam out in the cool water till my head felt cool as the water: then turned and swam back in, but the beach wasn't deserted completely any longer. There was a very old gentleman on it. He called 'Help!' to me, as if he was in the water drowning, and I was on shore. I swam in and asked him how I could help him and he said this, he said: 'Help me out there, I can't make it alone, I've gone past pain I can bear.' – I could see it was true. He was elegantly dressed but emaciated, cadaverous. I gave him the help he wanted, I led him out in the water, it wasn't easy. Once he started to panic, I had to hold on to him tight as a lover till he got back his courage and said, All right, the tide took him as light as a leaf. But just before I did that, and this is the oddest thing, he took out his wallet and thrust all the money in it into my hand. Here take this, he said to me. And I –

MRS GOFORTH: Took it, did you, you took it?

CHRIS: The sea had no use for his money. The fish in the sea had no use for it, either, so I took it and went on where I was going.

MRS GOFORTH: How much were you paid for this – service?

CHRIS: It was a very special difficult service: I was well paid for it.

MRS GOFORTH: Did you tell the old Hindu, the Swami, when you got to his place, that you'd killed an old man on the way and –

CHRIS: I told him that I had helped a dying old man to get through it.

MRS GOFORTH: What did he say about that?

CHRIS [*reflectively*]: What did he say: – He said, You've found your vocation: and he smiled. It was a beautiful smile in spite of showing bare gums, and – he held out his hand for the money: the hand was beautiful too in spite of being dry skin pulled tight as a glove over bones.

MRS GOFORTH: Did you give him the money?

CHRIS: Yes, they needed the money: I didn't: I gave it to them.

MRS GOFORTH: I *bet* you did.

CHRIS: I *did*.

MRS GOFORTH: Did he say thank you for it?

CHRIS: I don't know if he did. You see, they – No, I guess you don't see. – They had a belief in believing that too much is said when feeling, quiet feelings – enough. – Says *more* . . .

　　And he had a gift for gesture. You couldn't believe how a hand that shrivelled and splotched could make such a beautiful gesture of holding out the hand to be helped from the ground. It made me, so quickly, peaceful. That was important to me, that sudden feeling of quiet, because I'd come there, all the way down there, with the – the spectre of lunacy at my heels all the way. – He said: Stay. – We sat about a fire on the beach that night: Nobody said anything.

MRS GOFORTH: No message, he didn't have any message?

CHRIS: Yes, that night it was silence, it was the meaning of silence.

MRS GOFORTH: Silence? Meaning?

CHRIS: Acceptance.

MRS GOFORTH: What of?

CHRIS: Oh, many things, everything, nearly. Such as how to live and to die in a way that's more dignified than most of us know how to do it. And of how not to be frightened of not knowing what isn't meant to be known, acceptance of not knowing anything but the moment of still existing until we stop existing, and acceptance of that moment, too.

MRS GOFORTH: How do you know he wasn't just an old faker?

CHRIS: How do you know that I am not just a young one?

MRS GOFORTH: I don't. You *are* what they call you!

[*He takes hold of her hand.*]

CHRIS: As much as anyone is what anyone calls him.

MRS GOFORTH: A butcher is called a butcher, and that's what he is. A baker is called a baker, and he's a baker. A –

CHRIS: Whatever they're called, they're *men*, and being men, they're not known by themselves or anyone else.

[*She presses a button that shrills on the stage.*]

MRS GOFORTH: Rudy? Rudy!

CHRIS: Your bodyguard's gone, Mrs Goforth.

[*She goes on pressing the button.*]

He left with the contents of your strong-box, your safe.

MRS GOFORTH: – I've got on me all my important jewels, and if Rudy's gone, I want you to go, too. Go on to your next appointment. You've tired me, you've done me in. This day has been the most awful day of my life . . .

CHRIS: I know: that's why you need me here a while longer.

[*He places his arm about her.*]

MRS GOFORTH: *Don't, don't* you – *scare* me!

CHRIS: Let me take you into your bedroom, now, and put you to bed, Mrs Goforth.

MRS GOFORTH: *No, no* GO, *let me* GO!!

[*He releases her: picks up his canvas sack.*]

Hey!

[*He pauses with his back to her.*]

– Did somebody tell you I was dying this summer? Yes, isn't that why you came here, because you imagined that I'd be ripe for a soft touch because I'm dying this summer? Come on, for once in your life be honestly frank, be frankly honest with someone! You've been tipped off that old Flora Goforth is about to go forth this summer.

CHRIS: – Yes, that's why I came here.

MRS GOFORTH: – Well, I've escorted four husbands to the eternal threshold and come back alone without them, just with the loot of *three* of them, and, ah, God, it was like I was building a shell of bone round my heart with their goddam loot, their loot the material for it. – It's my turn, now, to go forth, and I've got no choice but to do it. But I'll do it alone. I don't want to be escorted, I want to go forth alone. But you, you counted on touching my heart because you'd heard I was dying, and old dying people are your speciality, your vocation. But you miscalculated with this one. This milk train doesn't stop here anymore. I'll give you some practical advice. Go back to Naples. Walk along Santa Lucia, the bay-front. Yesterday, there, they smelt the smell of no money, and treated you like a used, discarded used person. It'll be different this time. You'll probably run into some Americans at a sidewalk table along there, a party that's in for some shopping from the islands. If you're lucky, they'll ask you to sit down with them and say, 'Won't you have something, Chris?' – Well, *have* something, Chris! and if you play your cards right, they might invite you to go back to an island with them. Your best bet is strangers, I guess. Don't work on the young ones or anybody attractive. They're not ripe to be taken, and not the old ones, either, they been taken too often. Work on the middleage drunks, that's who to work on, Chris, work on them, sometimes the old milk train still comes to a temporary stop at their crazy station, so concentrate on the middleage drunks in Naples.

CHRIS: This isn't the time for such – practical advice . . .

[*She makes a gasping sound and presses a tissue to her mouth, turning upstage.*]

MRS GOFORTH [*turning front*]: – A paper rose . . . [*The tissue is dyed red with blood.*] – Before you go, help me into my bedroom, I can't make it alone . . .

[*He conducts her to the screen between the two rooms as the* STAGE ASSISTANTS *advance from the wings to remove it.*]

– It's full of historical treasures. The chandelier, if the dealer that sold it to me wasn't a liar, used to hang in Versailles, and the bed, if he wasn't lying, was the bed of Countess Walewska, Napoleon's Polish mistress, it's a famous old bed, for a famous old body . . .

[*The* STAGE ASSISTANTS *remove the screen masking the bed.*]

CHRIS: Yes, it looks like the catafalque of an empress. [*He lifts her on to the bed, and draws a cover over her.*]
MRS GOFORTH: *Don't leave me alone till –*
CHRIS: I never leave till the end.

[*She stretches out her blind, jewelled hand, He takes it.*]

MRS GOFORTH: *– Not so tight, the –*
CHRIS: I know, the rings cut your fingers.

[*He draws a ring off a finger. She gasps. He draws off another. She gasps again.*]

MRS GOFORTH: Be here, when I wake up.

[*Then the* STAGE ASSISTANTS *place before her the bed screen with the gold-winged griffin cresting its middle panel. Light dims out on that area and is brought up on the turning mobile. Music seems to come from the turning mobile that casts very delicate gleams of light on the stage.*

BLACKIE *appears on the forestage as the* STAGE ASSISTANTS *bring out a dinner-table and rapidly set two places. Then they cross to the flag-staff by the right wings and begin to slowly lower the flag.*]

ONE: Flag-lowering ceremony on the late Mrs Goforth's mountain.
TWO: Bugle?

[*A muted bugle is heard, as if from a distance.*]

– That's not Taps, that's Reveille.
ONE: It's Reveille always, Taps never, for the gold griffin.
TWO [*Snapping his fingers*]: Let's go.

[*Exeunt with folded banner.*

CHRIS *comes from behind the bedroom screen, on to the terrace where* BLACKIE *sits coolly waiting.*

The STAGE ASSISTANTS *reappear in mess-jackets bearing a small table set for supper on the terrace: they place it before* BLACKIE: *she rises and pours wine into a medieval goblet as she speaks to* CHRIS.]

BLACKIE: – Is it – is she –?

[CHRIS *nods as he moves out on to the forestage.*]

BLACKIE: Was it what they call 'peaceful'?

[CHRIS *nods again.*]

With all that fierce life in her?

CHRIS: You always wonder afterwards where it's gone, so far, so quickly. You feel it must be still around somewhere, in the air. But there's no sign of it.

BLACKIE: Did she say anything to you before she –?

CHRIS: She said to me: 'Be here when I wake up.' – After I'd taken her hand and stripped the rings off her fingers.

BLACKIE: What did you do with –?

CHRIS [*giving her a quick look that might suggest an understandable shrewdness*]: – Under her pillow like a pharaoh's breakfast waiting for the pharaoh to wake up hungry . . .

[*She comes up beside him on the forestage and offers him the wine-goblet. The sea is heard under the mountain.*]

BLACKIE: The sea is saying the name of your next mobile.

CHRIS: BOOM!

BLACKIE: What does it mean?

CHRIS: It says 'Boom' and that's what it means: no translation, no explanation, just 'BOOM'.

[*He drinks from the goblet and passes it back to her as –*]

THE CURTAIN FALLS SLOWLY

Small Craft Warnings

To Bill Barnes:
You said to go on, and I went.

Too Personal?*

The greatest danger, professionally, of becoming the subject of so many 'write-ups' and personal appearances on TV and lecture platforms is that the materials of your life, which are, in the case of all organic writing, the materials of your work, are sort of telegraphed in to those who see you and to those who read about you. So, when you get to the serious organization of this material into your work, people (meaning audiences and critics – all but the few most tolerant whom you naturally regard as the best) have a sort of *déjà vu* or *déjà entendu* reaction to these materials which you have submitted to the cathartic process of your 'sullen craft and art'.

You may justifiably wonder why a man of my years in his profession, recognizing this hazard, has yet been willing to expose himself (with a frequency which seems almost symptomatic of clinical exhibitionism) to all of these interviews and the fewer, but equally personal, exposures on platform and 'the tube'.

I can offer you at least two reasons for this phenomenon. One is probably something with which you will immediately empathize. When one has passed through an extensive period of that excess of privacy which is imposed upon a person drifting almost wilfully out of contact with the world, anticipating that final seclusion of the non-being, there comes upon him, when that period wears itself out and he is still alive, an almost insatiable hunger for recognition of the fact that he is, indeed, still alive, both as man and artist. That's reason number one. The other is rather comical, I'm afraid. You get a devastatingly bad write-up, and you feel that you are washed up for good.

* This was meant to be submitted to the *New York Times* as a pre-opening piece, but they chose to interview me instead – T.W.

Then some magazine editor gets through to you on that phone in the studio of your tropical retreat, the phone that you never pick up till it's rung so persistently that you assume that your secretary and house guests have been immobilized by nerve gas or something of that nature, and this editor speaks to you as sympathetically as the family doctor to a child stricken with a perforated appendix and tells you that he is as shocked as you were by the tasteless exposé-type of interview which appeared about you in a recent issue of some other mag. And then, of course, you forget about work, and you rage yourself into a slather over the iniquities and duplicities of the 'interviewer' referred to. You say, 'Why, that creature was so drunk he didn't know what street I lived on, and the guy that set me up for him laced my martini with sodium pentathol, and all I remember about this occasion is that my head came off my shoulders and hit the ceiling and I heard myself babbling away like an hysteric and I hadn't the slightest notion that he had a concealed tape recorder with him, and later he offered to play bridge with me that night, and he came over again with the tape recorder in some orifice of his body, I presume, and you know I do not see well and you know I like to hold forth to apparently amiable listeners, and I just assume that when they say "I am interested only in your work", that that's what they mean.'

Now the editor has you on the hook.

'That's exactly my reaction to the revolting piece and how about letting us do a piece to correct it?'

You grasp at this offer like a drowning rat climbs on to anything that will float it. So you get another write-up. Then after this write-up, which is usually more colourful and better written than the one before, but equally non-serious, if not downright clownish, you feel that it is a life-or-death matter, professionally, with a new play opening somewhere, to correct the hilarious misquotes and exaggerations which embellished the second write-up, and so you go on to others and others. Now at last you have poured out, compulsively and perhaps fatally, all the recent content of your experience which should have been held in reserve for its proper place, which is in the work you're doing every morning (which, in my case, is the writing I do every morning).

Is it or is it not right or wrong for a playwright to put his persona into his work?

My answer is: 'What else can he do?' – I mean the very root-necessity of all creative work is to express those things most involved in his experience. Otherwise, is the work, however well executed, not a manufactured, a synthetic thing? I've said, perhaps repeatedly, that I have two major classifications for writing: that which is organic and that which is not. And this opinion still holds.

Now let me attempt to entertain you once more with an anecdote.

Long ago, in the early forties, I attended a very posh party given by the Theatre Guild. I was comfortably and happily seated at a small table with my dear friend Miss Jo Healy, who was receptionist at the Guild in those days, when a lady with eyes that blazed with some nameless frenzy rushed up to me like a guided missile and seized me by the arm and shrieked to me, 'You've got to meet Miss Ferber, she's dying to meet you.'

Now in those days I was at least pliable, and so I permitted myself to be hauled over to a large table at which were seated a number of Diamond T trucks disguised as ladies.

'Oh, Miss Ferber,' shrieked my unknown pilot, 'this is Tennessee Williams.'

Miss Ferber gazed slowly up and delivered this annihilating one-liner:

'The best that I can manage is a mild "Yippee".'

'Madam,' I said, 'I can't even manage that.'

Now everyone knows, who is cognizant of the world of letters, that Miss Edna Ferber was a creature of mammoth productivity and success. She was good at doing her thing; her novel and picture sales are fairly astronomical, I would guess.

I bring her up because she represents to me the classic, the archetypal, example of a writer whose work is impersonal, at least upon any recognizable level. I cannot see her in the oil fields of Texas with Rock Hudson and the late James Dean. Nor can I see her in any of her other impressive epics. I see her only as a lady who chose to put down a writer who was then young and vulnerable with such a gratuitously malicious one-liner. I mean without provocation, since I had literally been dragged to the steps of her throne.

So far I have spoken only in defence of the personal kind of writing. Now I assure you that I know it can be overdone. It is the responsibility of the writer to put his experience as a being into work that refines it and elevates it and that makes of it an essence that a wide audience can somehow manage to feel in themselves: 'This is true.'

In all human experience, there are parallels which permit common understanding in the telling and hearing, and it is the frightening responsibility of an artist to make what is directly or allusively close to his own being communicable and understandable, however disturbingly, to the hearts and minds of all whom he addresses.

T.W.
26 MARCH 1972

The Cast

The first English production of this play was at the Hampstead Theatre Club, London, on 29 January 1973. It was directed by Vivian Matalon; the stage setting and costumes were by Saul Radomsky, lighting by Robert Ornbo. On 13 March 1973, the production was transferred to the Comedy Theatre, London. The cast was as follows:

LEONA DAWSON	*Elaine Stritch*
MONK	*Peter Jones*
DOC	*George Pravda*
BILL	*Edward Judd*
VIOLET	*Frances De La Tour*
STEVE	*James Berwick*
QUENTIN	*Tony Beckley*
BOBBY	*Eric Deacon*
TONY, THE COP	*John Bay*

Act One: A bar along the Southern California Coast
Act Two: An hour or two later

Act One

The curtain rises. The sound of ocean wind is heard. The stage is lighted at a very low level.

The scene is a somewhat non-realistic evocation of a bar on the beach-front in one of those coastal towns between Los Angeles and San Diego. It attracts a group of regular patrons who are nearly all so well known to each other that it is like a community club, and most of these regulars spend the whole evening there. Ideally, the walls of the bar, on all three sides, should have the effect of fog rolling in from the ocean. A blue neon outside the door says: 'Monk's Place'. The bar runs diagonally from upstage to down; over it is suspended a large varnished sailfish, whose gaping bill and goggle-eyes give it a constant look of amazement. There are about three tables, with red-checked tablecloths. Stage right there is a juke box, and in the wall at right are doors to the ladies' and gents' lavatories. A flight of stairs ascends to the bar-owner's living quarters. The stairs should be masked above the first few steps.

The bar interior is dimly, evenly lit at rise. At some time in the course of the play, when a character disengages himself from the group to speak as if to himself, the light in the bar should dim, and a special spot should illuminate each actor as he speaks.

MONK *is behind the bar serving* DOC. MONK, *the bar-owner, and* DOC, *who lost his licence for heavy drinking but still practises more or less clandestinely, are middle-aged.*

At a downstage table sits VIOLET, *at her feet a battered suitcase fastened with a rope. Her eyes are too large for her face, and they are usually moist;*

her appearance suggests a derelict kind of existence; still, she has about her a pale, bizarre sort of beauty. As LEONA DAWSON later puts it, she's like a water plant.

MONK [to DOC]: Notice? [He nods his head.] Over there?

> [DOC emerges from introspection to glance the way indicated by MONK. They both gaze at VIOLET.]

VIOLET [singing a bit, self-conscious under their scrutiny]:
The wheel of fortune
Keeps turning around . . .

> [She can't remember past this.]

DOC [voice filtered through booze]: Oh, yes, she's a noticeable thing. She has a sort of not-quite-with-it appearance. Amorphous, that's the word. Something more like a possibility than a completed creature.

MONK: What I mean is the *suitcase. With* her.

DOC: Oh, yes, the suitcase. Does she think she's in the waiting room of a depot?

MONK: I think she thinks she's moved in here.

DOC: Oh. That's a possible problem for you there.

MONK: You're Goddam right. I'm running a tavern that's licensed to dispense spirits, not a pad for vagrants. You see, they see those stairs. They know I live up there.

DOC: Yep, they see those stairs to the living quarters above, and it hits them dimly that you might need the solace of their companionship up there some nights when they find it convenient to offer it to you, and I don't need to tell you that this solace of companionship is not the least expensive item on the shelves of the fucking supermarket a man of my age has to spend what's left of his life in. Oh, that solace, that comfort of companionship is on the shelves of the market even for me, but I tell you, the price is inflated on it. I had me one last summer. Remember that plump little Chicano woman used to come in here with me some nights last summer? A little wet-leg woman, nice boobs on her and a national monument for an ass? Well, she came to me for medical attention.

[MONK *laughs heartily at this.*

BILL *enters the bar; he comes up to it with an over-relaxed amiability like a loser putting up a bold front: by definition a 'stud' – but what are definitions?*

MONK *mechanically produces* BILL's *can of Miller's but doesn't open it for him.*]

She had worms, diet of rotten beef tacos, I reckon, or tamales or something. I diagnosed it correctly. I gave her the little bottle and the wooden spoon and I said to her, 'Bring me in a sample of your stool for lab analysis.' She didn't know what I meant. Language barrier. I finally said, 'Señorita, bring a little piece of your shit in the bottle tomorrow.' [*He and* MONK *laugh heartily.*]

[BILL *is worried over the fact his beer can is not opened and served.*]

VIOLET: Hey, Bill . . .

DOC: Some beginning of some romance. Dewormed the lady and laid her in place of payment. Jesus, what a love story. I had her all summer, but in September she met a good-looking young pimp who made her critical of me. She called me a dirty old man, so I let her go.

BILL: Hey, Monk. About that beer.

MONK [*ignoring* BILL]: I don't remember you coming in here with a woman.

DOC: We always sat at a back table arguing over the fair expense of her ass.

BILL: Jesus, Monk, how big a tab has Leona run up here!? For Chrissake! [*He leans across the bar and snatches the can of Miller's from* MONK's *hand.* MONK *had ignored him only half deliberately and is annoyed by the grab.*]

MONK: Look, I don't run Leona's tab through a computer, since I know she's good for it. If you want the can opened, give it back here. [*He opens the can.*] Now if it was your tab, not hers, I'd worry, but since it's hers, not yours, I don't. O.K.? No offence, no complaint, just . . .

VIOLET: Bill?

BILL: I could tell you some things.

MONK: Why don't you tell 'em to Violet, she's called you three times.

BILL [*glancing at her*]: Hi, Vi.

VIOLET: I had an awful experience today with Mr Menzies at the amusement arcade. [*Sobbing sound.*] Oh, I don't know what to do. Min broke in. Last night. Menzies said I . . . Come over here so I can tell you. Oh, and bring me a beer and a pepperoni, I'm famished. Lonesome and famished.

BILL: You want me to solve both those situations for you?

VIOLET: Yes, please.

BILL [*to* MONK]: Another Miller's and a coupla Slim Jims.

MONK: Yep, I got that message. Have you left Leona?

VIOLET: Bill, where's Leona?

BILL: Crying into a stew in her Goddam trailer.

[MONK *opens another beer, and* BILL *ambles over to* VIOLET *with the pepperonis and beer and the smile he meets the world with. It is a hustler's smile, the smile of a professional stud – now ageing a bit but still with considerable memorabilia of his young charm.*]

VIOLET: Thanks, Bill . . .

[MONK *is toying with a radio which is over the bar.*]

RADIO VOICE: Heavy seas from Point Conception south to the Mexican border, fog continuing till tomorrow noon, extreme caution should be observed on all highways along this section of the coastline.

MONK [*ironically, turning off radio*]: Small craft warnings, Doc.

DOC: That's right, Monk, and you're running a place of refuge for vulnerable human vessels, and . . .

VIOLET [*closer to* BILL]: Have you left Leona? For good?

BILL: Just till she gets her knickers out of that twist. She had this brother, a faggot that played the fiddle in church, and whenever she's drunk, she starts to cry up a storm about this little fag that she admitted was arrested for loitering in the Greyhound bus station men's room, and if I say. 'Well, he was asking for it,' she throws something at me.

VIOLET [*leaning amorously towards him*]: A man like you.

BILL: A man like me?

VIOLET: A bull of a man like you. You got arms on you big as the sides of a ham. [*She strokes his bare arm.*]

BILL: That ain't all I got big.

VIOLET: You mean what I think?

BILL: If you can't see you can feel.

[*She reaches under the table, and it is obvious that she is feeling him.*]

A man likes appreciation. Now I got a letter this week from a female guv'ment employee in Sacramento who's a Reagan supporter.

VIOLET: Huh?

BILL: Shit. She ain't seen me since '65 but remembers me clearly and wants me back on her aquabed with her, and if you've slept in an aquabed it don't matter who's in it with you.

[*The door bursts open.* LEONA *enters like a small bull making his charge into the ring.* LEONA, *a large, ungainly woman, is wearing white clam-digger slacks and a woolly pink sweater. On her head of dyed corkscrew curls is a sailor's hat which she occasionally whips off her head to slap something with – the bar, a tabletop, somebody's back – to emphasize a point. There are abrupt changes of position at the downstage table at her entrance, but she notices only* BILL *there.*]

LEONA: YOUUUUU ... MOTHER! I was talkin' to you from the stove and you weren't there!

[BILL *chuckles and winks.*]

Three hours I spent shopping for and preparing a ... memorial dinner while you watched TV.

BILL: Stew and veg.

LEONA [*lyrically, as a pop-poem*]: Lamb stew with garden fresh vegetables from the Farmer's Market, seasoned with bay leaves, and rosemary and thyme.

BILL: Stew.

LEONA: I'd set up a little banquet table in that trailer tonight, my grandmother's silver and Irish lace tablecloth, my crystal candlesticks with the vine leaves filigreed on 'em in silver which I'd polished, all spit-polished for this memorial dinner, set the candles on either side of my single rose vase containing a single talisman rose just opened, a table like a photo from *House and Garden*. I talk from the stove to no one. I open the fridge to get out the jellied bouillon, madrilene, topped with . . . 'Okayyyy, ready.' I come in and I'm received by the TV set and the trailer door hanging open, and in the confusion I knock over and break my cut-glass decanter of Burgundy, imported.

BILL: I went out for a bottle. You'd kilt a fifth of Imp. She was crying in the stew to save on salt.

LEONA: Without word or a note on the table. You went! Why? For what?

VIOLET: Leona, Bill's not happy tonight, so let him be.

LEONA: Two people's not happy and one of 'em with *reason!* Is that your suitcase with you? Are you thrown out, evicted? A lady of the street? Oh, my God, here's a good one I heard at the shop today about a pair of street-ladies in Dublin. One enters a pub, elegant but pissed, and she says to the barman, 'Two gins for two ladies.' He observes her condition and says, 'Where is the other lady?' 'The other lady,' she says, 'is in the gutter resting.' [*Only she is amused by the story.*] Oh, well, I thought it was funny. [LEONA *sits at table with* VIOLET *and* BILL.] Violet, dear, will you look at your nails?

VIOLET: I know, the enamel's chipping.

LEONA: Yes! Exposing the dirt.

[*Violet drops her hands under the table.*]

Oh, my God, forget it, forget the whole enchilada. Not worth a thought.

[*No response.*]

Excuse me a moment. I'm going to press one button three times on that multiselector, and Violet, here's an orange stick for your nails . . . Don't be depressed. A sure cure for depression is the axe.

VIOLET: I'm not depressed.

LEONA [*laughing*]: Then you must not be conscious. [*She crosses to the juke box.*] I hope nobody objects to the number I play. It's going to be played here repeatedly tonight, appreciated or not. [*She bends over the juke box to find the desired number, which she herself contributed to the 'Classicals' on the box.*] Rock? No! Popular? No! Classicals – yes! Number? Number? Which?

VIOLET: Tell her I'm not depressed.

[VIOLET's *hand has dropped under the table. It is apparent that she is reaching for* BILL.]

BILL: *She's* depressed . . . and depressing. [*Leans back luxuriously in a chair. A look to* LEONA. *He speaks with emphasis, rather than volume.*] . . . Not bad, huh? A definite . . . personal . . . asset?

[MONK *turns up radio. Gets static.*]

LEONA: Do you have to turn that on when I'm . . .

[*At this precise moment she is caught by the change in attitudes at the downstage table. Her eyes widen; her hands clench; she takes a couple of paces towards the table and crouches a bit to peer under it. Then quick as a shot:*]

YOUUU CUNT!

[*She charges.*
    Violet screams and springs up, overturning her chair.]

MONK: Hold her!

[BILL's *massive frame obstructs* LEONA, *not only her motion but her view of* VIOLET. BILL *is holding her by both shoulders, grinning into her face.*
    The following lines overlap.]

LEONA: OFF HANDS!
MONK: Nope, nope, nope, nope, nope!
LEONA: McCorkle, DON' YOU . . . !
MONK: Keep her at that table!

[*During this* MONK *has crossed from behind the bar.*

VIOLET *has turned about dizzily, then fled into the ladies'*.

LEONA *stamps on* BILL'*s foot. He yells, falls back an instant, releasing her. As she rushes forward, he gives her a hard slap on the butt; she turns to give him battle, and is caught from behind by* MONK. *She kicks at* MONK'*s shin, and gives* BILL *a wallop in the face with her cap.*]

BILL [*rubbing his eyes*]: Goddam, she . . .

MONK: I'm havin' no violence here! Never! None! From no one!

[*A sudden hush falls: a sudden moment of stillness in a* corrida.]

LEONA [*incredulously, profoundly, hurtly, right into* BILL'*s face*]: YOU! Let *her*! In front of me? . . . in PUBLIC! . . . In a BAR!

BILL: What the fuck of it! You hit me right in the eyes with . . .

LEONA [*makes a big-theatre turn and shouts*]: Where IS she? Where's she gone? [*Receiving no answer – there is still no sound from* VIOLET'*s place of refuge – she suddenly rushes for the stairs.*]

MONK: Nobody's up my stairs! Come down those . . .

[VIOLET'*s lamentation begins.*]

LEONA: Aw! She's gone to the LADIES'! Change the name on that door.

MONK: I'm operating a place for gents and ladies. [*He is panting a bit.*]

LEONA: Gents and . . . what?

MONK: Ladies.

LEONA: Aw, now, Monk. I thought you run a clean place but don't come on with . . . her? Lady? Him? Gent? [*She points towards the ladies' room and then towards* BILL.] There's limits to . . .

MONK: Yes. Stay away from . . .

[LEONA *had started towards the ladies'*. MONK *blocks her. She throws her head back and utters an apocalyptic outcry. It's like the outcry of all human protest.*]

No more disturbance of . . .

LEONA [*drawing herself up heroically as she confronts* MONK *almost nose-to-nose*]: LET ME SET YOU STRAIGHT ABOUT WHAT'S A LADY! A lady's a woman, with respect for herself and for relations of others! HER? IN THERE? WAILING? RESPECT FOR? . . . She's got no respect for herself and that is the single respect in which she's correct to! No one could blame her for that! [*She has resumed her pacing and slapping at things with her sailor's cap.*] What could she possibly find to respect in herself? She lives like an animal in a room with no bath that's directly over the amusement arcade at the foot of the pier, yeah, right over the billiards, the pinball games, and the bowling alleys at the amusement arcade, it's bang, bang, bang, loud as a TV western all day and all night, and then bang, bang again at eight a.m. It would drive a sane person crazy but she couldn't care less. She don't have a closet, she didn't have a bureau so she hangs her dresses on a piece of rope that hangs across a corner between two nails, and her other possessions she keeps on the floor in boxes.

BILL: What business is it of yours?

LEONA: None, not a Goddam bit! When she was sick? I went there to bring her a chicken. I asked her, where is your silver? She didn't have any silver, not a fork, spoon, or knife, hell, not even a plate, but she ate the chicken, aw, yeah, she ate the chicken like a dog would eat it, she picked it up in her paws and gnawed at it just like a dog. Who came to see if she was living or dead? ME! ONLY! I got her a bureau, I got her a knife, fork, and spoon, I got her china, I got her a change of bed linen for her broken-down cot, and ev'ry day after work I come by that Goddam rathole with a bottle of hot beef bouillon or a chicken or meatloaf to see what she needed and bring it, and then one time I come by there to see what she needed and bring it. The bitch wasn't there. I thought my God she's died or they put her away. I run downstairs, and I heard her screaming with joy in the amusement arcade. She was having herself a ball with a shipload of drunk sailor boys; she hardly had time to speak to me.

BILL: Maybe she'd gotten sick of you. That's a possible reason.

LEONA: It's a possible reason I was sick of her, too, but I'd thought that the bitch was dying of malnutrition, and I thought she was human, and a human life is worth saving or what the shit *is* worth saving. But is she human? She's just a parasite creature, not even made out of flesh but out of wet biscuit dough, she always looks like the bones are dissolving in her.

BILL [*banging his beer bottle on the table*]: DO YOU THINK I BELONG TO YOU? I BELONG TO MYSELF, I JUST BELONG TO MYSELF.

LEONA: Aw, you pitiful piece of ... worthless ... conceit! [*She addresses the bar.*] ... Never done a lick of work in his life ... He has a name for his thing. He calls it Junior. He says he takes care of Junior and Junior takes care of him. How long is that gonna last? How long does he figure Junior is going to continue to provide for him, huh? HUH! ... Forever or *less* than forever? ... Thinks the sun rises and sets between his legs and that's the reason I put him in my trailer, feed him, give him beer-money, pretend I don't notice there's five or ten bucks less in my pocketbook in the morning than my pocketbook had in it when I fell to sleep, night before.

BILL: Go out on the beach and tell that to the sea gulls, they'd be more int'rested in it.

VIOLET [*shrilly, from the ladies' room*]: Help me, help me, somebody, somebody call the po-liiiiice!

LEONA: Is she howling out the ladies' room window?

VIOLET: How long do I have to stay in here before you get the police?

LEONA: If that fink is howling out the ladies' room window, I'm going out back and throw a brick in at her.

MONK: Leona, now cool it, Leona.

LEONA: I'll pay the damage, I'll pay the hospital expenses.

MONK: Leona, why don't you play your violin number on the box and settle down at a table and ...

LEONA: When I been insulted by someone, I don't settle down at a table, or nowhere, NOWHERE!

[VIOLET *sobs and wails as* STEVE *comes into the bar.* STEVE *is wearing a floral-patterned sports shirt under a tan jacket and the greasy white trousers of a short-order cook.*]

STEVE: Is that Violet in there?

LEONA: Who else do you think would be howling out the ladies' room window but her, and you better keep out of this, this is between her and me.

STEVE: What happened? Did you hit Violet?

LEONA: You're Goddam right I busted that filthy bitch in the kisser, and when she comes out of the ladies', if she ever comes out, I'm gonna bust her in the kisser again, and kiss my ass, I'm just the one that can do it! MONK! DRINK! BOURBON SWEET!

MONK: Leona, you're on a mean drunk, and I don't serve liquor to no one on a mean drunk.

LEONA: Well, you can kiss it, too, you monkey-faced mother. [*She slaps the bar top with her sailor hat.*]

STEVE: Hey, did you hit Violet?

[BILL *laughs at this anticlimactic question.*]

LEONA: Have you gone deaf, have you got wax in your ears, can't you hear her howling in there? Did I hit Violet? The answer is yes, and I'm not through with her yet. [LEONA *approaches the door of the ladies' room.*] COME ON OUT OF THERE, VIOLET, OR I'LL BREAK IN THE DOOR! [*She bangs her fist on the door, then slaps it contemptuously with her cap, and resumes her pacing.*]

[BILL *keeps grinning and chuckling.*]

STEVE: Why did she hit Violet?

LEONA: Why don't you ask *me* why?

STEVE: Why did you hit Violet?

LEONA: I hit Violet because she acted indecent with that son of a bitch I been supporting for six months in my trailer.

STEVE: What do you mean 'indecent'?

LEONA: Jesus, don't you know her habits? Are you unconscious ev'ry night in this bar and in her rathole over the amusement arcade? I mean she acted indecent with her hands on the table. The red enamel had nearly all chipped off the nails and the fingernails, black, I mean *black*, like she'd spent every day for a month without washing her hands after making mud-pies with filthy motherless kids, and I thought to myself, it's awful, the degradation a woman can sink down into without respect for herself, so I said to her, Violet, will you look at your hands, will you look at your fingernails, Violet?

STEVE: Is that why you hit Violet?

LEONA: Goddam it, NO! Will you listen? I told her to look at her nails and she said, oh, the enamel is peeling, I know. I mean the dirtiness of the nails was not a thing she could notice, just the chipped red enamel.

STEVE: Is that why you hit Violet?

LEONA: Shit, will you shut up till I tell you why I hit her? I wouldn't hit her just for being unclean, unsanitary. I wouldn't hit her for nothing that affected just her. And now, if you'll pay attention, I'm going to tell you exactly why I did hit her. I got up from the table to play 'Souvenir'.

STEVE: What is the talking about? What are you talking about?

LEONA: When I come back to the table her hands had disappeared off it. I thought to myself, I'm sorry, I made her ashamed of her hands and she's hiding them now.

STEVE: Is that why you hit Violet?

LEONA: Why do you come in a bar when you're already drunk? No! Listen! It wasn't embarrassment over her filthy nails that had made her take her hands off the table top, it was her old habit, as filthy as her nails. The reason her pitiful hands had disappeared off the table was because under the table she was acting indecent with her hands in the lap of that ape that moved himself into my trailer and tonight will move himself out as fast as he moved himself in. And now do you know why I hit her? If you had balls, which it doesn't look like you do, you would've hit her yourself instead of making me do it.

STEVE: I wasn't there when it happened, but that's the reason you hit her?

LEONA: Yeah, now the reason has got through the fog in your head, which is thick as the fog on the beach.

[VIOLET *wails from the ladies' room.*]

STEVE: I'm not married to Violet, I never was or will be. I just wanted to know who hit her and why you hit her.

LEONA [*slapping at him with her cap*]: Annhh!

STEVE: Don't slap at me with that cap. What do I have to do with what she done or she does?

LEONA: No responsibility? No affection? No pity? You stand there hearing her wailing in the ladies' and deny there's any connection between you? Well, now I feel sorry for her. I regret that I hit her. She can come back out now and I won't hit her again. I see her life, the awfulness of her hands reaching out under a table, automatically creeping under a table into the lap of anything with a thing that she can catch hold of. Let her out of the ladies', I'll never hit her again. I feel too much pity for her, but I'm going out for a minute to breathe some clean air and to get me a drink where a barman's willing to serve me, and then I'll come back to pay up whatever I owe here and say good-bye to the sailfish, hooked and shellacked and strung up like a flag over . . . over . . . lesser, much lesser . . . creatures that never, ever sailed an inch in their . . . lives . . .

[*The pauses at the end of this speech are due to a shift of her attention towards a young man and a boy who have entered the bar. Her eyes have followed them as they walked past her to a table in the front. She continues speaking, but now as if to herself.*]

. . . When I leave here tonight, none of you will ever see me again. I'm going to stop by the shop, let myself in with my passkey and collect my own equipment, which is enough to open a shop of my own, write a good-bye note to Flo, she isn't a bad old bitch, I doubled her trade since I been there, she's going to miss me, poor Flo, then leave my passkey and cut back to my trailer and pack like lightning and move on to . . .

BILL: Where?

LEONA: Where I go next. You won't know, but you'll know I went fast.

[*Now she forgets her stated intention of going out of the bar and crosses to the table taken by the young man and the boy. The boy, BOBBY, wears faded jeans and a sweatshirt on the back of which is lettered 'Iowa to Mexico'. The young man, QUENTIN, is dressed effetely in a yachting jacket, maroon linen slacks, and a silk neck-scarf. Despite this costume, he has a quality of sexlessness, not effeminacy. Some years ago, he must have been remarkably handsome. Now his face seems to have been burned thin by a fever that is not of the flesh.*]

LEONA [*suddenly very amiable*]: Hi, boys!
QUENTIN: Oh. Hello. Good evening.
BOBBY [*with shy friendliness*]: Hello.

[*BILL is grinning and chuckling. VIOLET's weeping in the ladies' room no longer seems to interest anyone in the bar.*]

LEONA [*to BOBBY*]: How's the corn growing out there where the tall corn grows?
BOBBY: Oh, it's still growing tall.
LEONA: Good for the corn. What town or city are you from in Iowa?
BOBBY: Goldenfield. It's close to Dubuque.
LEONA: Dubuque, no shoot? I could recite the telephone book of Dubuque, but excuse me a minute, I want to play a selection on the number selector, and I'll come right back to discuss Dubuque with you. Huh? [*She moves as if totally pacified to the juke box and removes some coins from a pocket. They fall to the floor. She starts to bend over to pick them up, then decides not to bother, gives them a slight kick, gets a dollar bill out of a pocket, calling out:*] Monk, gimme change for a buck. [*LEONA crosses to MONK at bar, waving a dollar bill.*]
QUENTIN: Barman? . . . Barman? . . . What's necessary to get the barman's attention here, I wonder.

[*LEONA crosses back to juke box, stage right. BOBBY hands LEONA the change he's picked up off the floor. She looks for a number on the juke box.*]

MONK: I heard you. You've come in the wrong place. You're looking for the Jungle Bar, half a mile up the beach.

QUENTIN: Does that mean you'd rather not serve us?

MONK: Let me see the kid's draft card.

BOBBY: I just want a Coke.

QUENTIN: He wants a plain Coca-Cola, I'd like a vodka and tonic.

[LEONA *lights up the juke box with a coin and selects a violin number, 'Souvenir'. A look of ineffable sweetness appears on her face, at the first note of music.*]

BILL: Y' can't insult 'em, there's no way to bring 'em down except to beat 'em and roll 'em.

[*The bar starts to dim, and a special spot comes up on* BILL. *The violin music on the juke box plays softly under.*]

I noticed him stop at the door before he come in. He was about to go right back out when he caught sight of me. Then he decided to stay. A piss-elegant one like that is asking for it. After a while, say about fifteen minutes, I'll go in the gents' and he'll follow me in there for a look at Junior. Then I'll have him hooked. He'll ask me to meet him outside by his car or at the White Castle. It'll be a short wait and I don't think I'll have t'do more than scare him a little. I don't like beating 'em up. They can't help the way they are. Who can? Not me. Left home at fifteen, and like Leona says, I've never done a lick of work in my life and I never plan to, not as long as Junior keeps batting on the home team, but my time with Leona's run out. She means to pull out of here and I mean to stay . . .

[*The bar is relighted.* LEONA *is still at the juke box. She is leaning against the juke box, listening intently to the music.*]

MONK [*rapping at the ladies'*]: Violet, you can come out, now, she's playing that violin number.

[BILL *and* STEVE *laugh. The bar starts to dim, and a special spot comes up on* STEVE. *The violin number still plays under.*]

STEVE: I guess Violet's a pig, all right, and I ought to be ashamed to go around with her. But a man unmarried, forty-seven years old, employed as a short-order cook at a salary he can barely get by on alone, he can't be choosy. Nope, he has to be satisfied with the Goddam scraps in this world, and Violet's one of those scraps. She's a pitiful scrap, but . . . [*He shrugs sadly and lifts the beer bottle to his mouth.*] . . . something's better than nothing and I had nothing before I took up with her. She gave me a clap once and tried to tell me I got it off a toilet seat. I asked the doctor, is it possible to get a clap off a public toilet seat, and he said, yes, you can get it that way but you *don't.* [*He grins sadly and drinks again, wobbling slightly.*] . . . Oh, my life, my miserable, cheap life! It's like a bone thrown to a dog! I'm the dog, she's the bone. Hell, I know her habits. She's always down there in that amusement arcade when I go to pick her up, she's down there as close as she can get to some Navy kid, playing a pinball game, and one hand is out of sight. Hustling? I reckon that's it. I know I don't provide for her, just buy her a few beers here, and a hot dog on the way home. But, Bill, why's he let her mess around with him? One night he was braggin' about the size of his tool, he said all he had to do to make a living was wear tight pants on the street. Life! . . . Throw it to a dog. I'm not a dog, I don't want it. I think I'll sit at the bar and pay no attention to her when she comes out . . .

[*The light in the bar comes up to normal level as the spot fades out. After a moment,* VIOLET *comes out of the ladies' room slowly, with a piteous expression. She is dabbing her nostrils with a bit of toilet tissue. Her lips are pursed in sorrow so that she is like a travesty of a female saint under torture. She gasps and draws back a little at the sight of* LEONA; *then, discreetly sobbing, she edges on to a bar stool, and* MONK *gives her a beer.* STEVE *glares at her. She avoids looking at him.* BILL *grins and chuckles at his table.* LEONA *ignores the fact that* VIOLET *has emerged from her retreat. She goes on pacing the bar, but is enthralled by the music.*]

LEONA: My God, what an instrument, it's like a thing in your heart, it's a thing that's sad but better than being happy, in a . . . crazy drunk way . . .

VIOLET [*piteously*]: I don't know if I can drink, I feel sick at my stomach.

LEONA: Aw, shit, Violet. Who do you think you're kidding? You'll drink whatever is put in the reach of your paws. [*She slaps herself on the thigh with the sailor cap and laughs.*]

VIOLET: I do feel sick at my stomach.

LEONA: You're lucky you're sick at your stomach because your stomach can vomit, but when you're sick at your heart, that's when it's awful, because your heart can't vomit the memories of your lifetime. I wish my heart could vomit, I wish my heart could throw up the heartbreaks of my lifetime, my days in a beauty shop and my nights in a trailer. It wouldn't surprise me at all if I drove up to Sausalito alone this night. With no one . . .

[*She glances at* BILL, *who grins and chuckles.* VIOLET *sobs piteously again.* LEONA *gives* VIOLET *a fairly hard slap on the shoulders with her sailor's cap.* VIOLET *cries out in affected terror.*]

Shuddup, I'm not gonna hit you. Steve, take her off that bar stool and put her at a table, she's on a crying jag and it makes me sick.

STEVE [*to* VIOLET]: Come off it, Violet. Sit over here at a table, before you fall off the bar stool.

LEONA: She hasn't got a mark on her, not a mark, but she acts like I'd nearly kilt her, and turns to a weeping willow. But as for that ape that I put up in my trailer, I took him in because a life in a trailer, going from place to place any way the wind blows you, gets to be lonely, sometimes. But that's a mistake I'll not make again . . . knock wood! [*Knocks table top.*]

STEVE [*wishing to smooth troubled waters*]: Know what that means, to knock wood? It means to touch the wood of the true cross, Leona.

[*He peers gravely and nearsightedly into* LEONA's *face.*]

LEONA: Yeah, for luck, you need it.

MONK [*to* VIOLET *at bar*]: That's mine! Here's yours. [*She has reached out for* MONK's *drink.*]

STEVE: Violet, get off that stool and sit at a table.

LEONA You got to move her. She's got to be moved.

[STEVE *accepts this necessity. He supports* VIOLET'*s frail, liquid figure to a table upstage, but her long, thin arm snakes out to remove* MONK'*s drink from the bar top as she goes.*

The phone rings, and MONK *lifts it.*]

MONK: Monk's Place . . . Doc, it's for you.

DOC [*crossing to the end of the bar*]: Thanks, Monk.

MONK: The old Doc's worked up a pretty good practice for a man in retirement.

LEONA: Retirement your ass, he was kicked out of the medical profession for performing operations when he was so loaded he couldn't tell the appendix from the gizzard.

MONK: Leona, go sit at your table.

LEONA: You want responsibility for a human life, do you?

MONK: Bill, I think she's ready to go home now.

LEONA: I'll go home when I'm ready and I'll do it alone.

BILL: I seen a circus with a polar bear in it that rode a three-wheel bicycle. That's what you make me think of tonight.

LEONA: You want to know something, McCorkle? I could beat the shit out of you.

BILL: Set down somewhere and shut up.

LEONA: I got a suggestion for you. Take this cab fare . . . [*She throws a handful of silver on the table.*] . . . And go get your stuff out of my trailer. Clear it all out, because when I go home tonight and find any stuff of yours there, I'll pitch it out of the trailer and bolt the door on you. I'm just in the right mood to do it.

BILL: Don't break my heart.

LEONA: What heart? We been in my trailer together for six months and you contributed nothing.

BILL: Shit, for six months I satisfied you in your trailer!

LEONA: You never satisfied nothing but my mother complex. Never mind, forget it, it's forgotten. Just do this. Take this quarter and punch number K-6 three times on the juke box.

BILL: Nobody wants to hear that violin number again.

LEONA: I do, I'm somebody. My brother, my young brother, played it as good if not better than Heifetz on that box. Y'know, I look at you and I ask myself a question. How does it feel to've never had anything beautiful in your life and not even know you've missed it? [*She crosses towards the juke box.*] Walking home with you some night, I've said, Bill, look at the sky, will you look at that sky? You never looked up, just grunted. In your life you've had no experiation ... experience! Appreciation! ... of the beauty of God in the sky, so what is your life but a bottle of, can of, glass of ... one, two, three! [*She has punched the violin selection three times.*]

MONK: The Doc's still on the phone.

LEONA: 'Souvenir' is a soft number.

[*The violin number starts to play again on the juke box.*]

DOC [*returning to the bar*]: I've got to deliver a baby. Shot of brandy.

LEONA [*returning to BILL's table*]: It wouldn't be sad if you didn't know what you missed by coming into this world and going out of it some day without ever having a sense of, experience of and memory of, a beautiful thing in your life such as I have in mine when I remember the violin of and the face of my young brother.

BILL: You told me your brother was a fruit.

LEONA: I told you privately something you're repeating in public with words as cheap as yourself. My brother who played this number had pernicious anaemia from the age of thirteen and any fool knows a disease, a condition, like that would make any boy too weak to go with a woman, but he was so full of love he had to give it to someone like his music. And in my work, my profession as a beautician, I never seen skin or hair or eyes that could touch my brother's. His hair was a natural blond as soft as silk and his eyes were two pieces of heaven in a human face, and he played on the violin like he was making love to it. I cry! I cry! ... No, I don't, I *don't* cry! ... I'm proud that I've had something beautiful to remember as long as I live in my lifetime ...

[*VIOLET sniffles softly.*]

When they passed around the plate for the offering at church, they'd have him play in the choir stall and he played and he looked like an angel, standing under the light through the stained glass

window. Um-hummm. [*Her expression is rapt.*] ... And people,
even the tightwads, would drop paper money in the plates when
he played. Yes, always before the service, I'd give him a shampoo-
rinse so that his silky hair, the silkiest hair I've ever known on a
human head in my lifetime as a beautician, would look like an
angel's halo, touched with heavenly light. Why, people cried
like I'm crying and the preacher was still choked up when he
delivered the sermon. 'Angels of Light', that was it, the number
he played that Easter ... [*She sings a phrase of the song.*] Emotions of people can be worse than people but sometimes better
than people, yes, superior to them, and Haley had that gift of
making people's emotions uplifted, superior to them! But he got
weaker and weaker and thinner and thinner till one Sunday he
collapsed in the choir stall, and after that he failed fast, just faded
out of this world. Anaemia – pernicious ...

VIOLET [*sobbing*]: Anaemia, that's what I've got!

LEONA: Don't compare yourself to him, how dare you compare
yourself to him. He was too beautiful to live and so he died.
Otherwise we'd be living together in my trailer. I'd train him to
be a beautician, to bring out the homeliness in ... I mean the,
I mean the ... [*She is confused for a moment. She lurches into a bar
stool and knocks it over.*] I mean I'd train my young brother to lay
his hands on the heads of the homely and lonely and bring
some beauty out in them, at least for one night or one day or at
least for an hour. We'd have our own shop, maybe two of 'em,
and I wouldn't give you ... [*She directs herself to* BILL] ... the
time of the day, the time of the night, the time of the morning
or afternoon, the sight of you never would have entered my
sight to make me feel pity for you, no, noooo! [*She bends over*
BILL's *table, resting her spread palms on it, to talk directly into his
face.*] The companionship and the violin of my brother would
be all I had any need for in my lifetime till my death-time!
Remember this, Bill, if your brain can remember. Everyone
needs! One beautiful thing! In the course of a lifetime! To save
the heart from colluption!

BILL: What is 'colluption', fat lady?

LEONA: *CORRUPTION!* ... Without one beautiful thing in the course of a lifetime, it's all a death-time. A woman turns to a slob that lives with a slob, and life is disgusting to her and she's disgusting to life, and I'm just the one to . . .

BILL [*cutting in*]: If you'd rather live with a fruit . . .

LEONA: *Don't say it! Don't say it!* [*She seizes hold of a chair and raises it mightily over her head.* VIOLET *screams.* LEONA *hurls the chair to the floor.*] Shit, he's not worth the price of a broken chair! [*Suddenly she bursts into laughter that is prodigious as her anger or even more, it's like an unleashed element of nature. Several patrons of the bar, involuntarily, laugh with her. Abruptly as it started, the laughter stops short. There is total silence except for the ocean sound outside.*]

VIOLET: Steve, love, get me a hot dog with chili and onion, huh? Or maybe a Whopper.

STEVE: Oh, now you want a Whopper, a king-size burger, now, huh? Always got your hand out for something.

VIOLET: That's a cruel injustice. [*Sobs.*]

STEVE: Stop it!

VIOLET: I'm in paiii-in!

LEONA: Look at her, not a mark on her, but says she's in pain and wants a hot dog with everything on it, and I heard on TV that the Food Administration found insect and rodent parts in some hot dogs sold lately. [*She has been stalking the bar.*] Let her have him for supper! [*Indicates* BILL.]

DOC [*rising from his bar stool*]: Well, I better be going. Somebody's about to be born at Treasure Island.

LEONA: That's my trailer court where I keep my trailer. A baby's about to be born there?

BILL: Naw, not a baby, a full-grown adult's about to be born there, and that's why the Doc had t'brace himself with a coupla shots of brandy.

DOC [*turning about on his bar stool, glass in hand*]: You can't make jokes about birth and you can't make jokes about death. They're miracles, holy miracles, both, yes, that's what both of them are, even though, now, they're usually surrounded by . . . expedients that seem to take away the dignity of them. Birth? Rubber gloves, boiled water, forceps, surgical shears. And death? . . . The wheeze of an oxygen tank, the jab of a hypodermic needle to put out the panic light in the dying-out eyes, tubes in the arms and the kidneys, absorbent cotton inserted in the rectum to hold back the bowels discharged when the . . . the *being stops.* [*During this speech the bar dims, and a special spot comes up on* DOC.] . . . It's hard to see back of this cloud of . . . irreverent . . . paraphernalia. But behind them both are the holy mysteries of . . . birth and . . . death . . . They're dark as the face of a black man, yes, that's right, a Negro, yes. I've always figured that God is a black man with no light on his face, He moves in the dark like a black man, a Negro miner in the pit of a lightless coal mine, obscured completely by the . . . irrelevancies and irreverencies of public worship . . . standing to sing, kneeling to pray, sitting to hear the banalities of a preacher . . . Monk, did I give you my . . . ?

[*As light comes up in bar, the spot fades out.*]

MONK: Bag? Yeah, here. [MONK *hands a medical kit across the bar.*]

LEONA: I want to know, is nobody going to stop him from going out, in his condition, to deliver a baby? I want to know quick, or I'll stop him myself!

DOC: Thanks. And I'll have a shot of brandy to wash down a Benzedrine tablet to steady my hands.

LEONA: NOBODY, HUH?

DOC: Tonight, as I drove down Canyon Road, I noticed a clear bright star in the sky, and it was right over that trailer court, Treasure Island, where I'm going to deliver a baby. So now I know: I'm going to deliver a new Messiah tonight.

LEONA: The hell you are, you criminal, murdering quack, leggo of that bag!

[LEONA *rushes* DOC *and snatches his bag. She starts towards the door but is blocked by one of the men; starts in another direction and is blocked again. She is then warily approached from three or four sides by* MONK, DOC, BILL, *and* STEVE *as trainers approaching an angry 'big cat'.*

All ad-lib during this, and in the lines that follow, MONK, LEONA,

and DOC *speak almost simultaneously, while* STEVE *keeps up a con-
tinual placating repetition of 'Violet says' and 'Have a beer with us,
Leona.'*

*The effect should almost suggest a quartet in opera: several voices
blended but each pursuing its separate plaint.*]

MONK: Don't let her out with . . .
DOC: My bag! The instruments in that bag . . .
MONK: Steve, Bill, hold her, I can't with my . . .
DOC: Are worth and insured for . . . over two thousand! If you dam-
age the contents of that bag . . . I'll sue you for their value and for
slander!

[LEONA *sits on* DOC's *bag at center table.*]

LEONA: I'll surrender this bag to you in a courtroom only!
DOC: Very expensive, very, very expensive.
STEVE: Look, she's sitting on Doc's bag. Violet says she's, Leona, Vio-
let wants to, listen, listen, listen Leona, set down and have a beer
with us! Violet says she . . .
VIOLET: Not at this table, no, no, I'm scared of Leona, she . . .
STEVE: Violet, shuddup. Leona? Violet's offered you to a . . . drink!
Have a drink with us, Leona.
LEONA: I'll stay sitting on it till some action is taken to stop this man
from illegal . . .

[BILL *squirts a mouthful of beer at her, and she immediately leaps up
to strike at him fiercely with the sailor's cap. In that instant* MONK
seizes the bag from the chair and tosses it to DOC, *who rushes out the
door with it.*]

All of you are responsible! . . . If he murders a baby tonight and
the baby's mother! Is life worth nothing in here? I'm going out. I
am going to make a phone call.

[BILL *makes a move to stop her.*]

Don't you *dare* to! Try to!
MONK: Who're you going to call?

STEVE: Who's she going to call?

LEONA [to MONK]: That's my business, strictly. I'm not gonna use your phone. [She charges out the door, and the door is again left open on the sound of surf.]

MONK: What's she up to?

STEVE: What's she up to, Bill?

BILL [grinning and shrugging]: I know what she's up to. She's gonna call the office at Treasure Island and tell 'em the Doc's comin' out there to deliver a baby.

MONK: Well, stop her, go stop her!

STEVE: Yeh, you better stop her.

BILL [indifferently]: She's disappeared in the fog.

MONK: She can get the Doc into serious trouble, and his condition's no better than mine is . . .

BILL: Shit, they know her too well to pay any attention to her call.

MONK: I hate to eighty-six anyone out of my place; I never have done that in the six years I've run it, but I swear to God, I . . . have to avoid . . . disturbance.

VIOLET [plaintively]: Last week she gave me a perm and a rinse for nothing, and then tonight she turns on me, threatens to kill me.

BILL: Aw, she blows hot and cold, dependin' on whichever way her liquor hits her.

VIOLET: She's got two natures in her. Sometimes she couldn't be nicer. A minute later she . . .

MONK [at the telephone]: Shut up a minute. Treasure Island? This is Monk speaking from Monk's Place . . . Yeah. Now. If you get a phone call out there from Leona Dawson, you know her, she's got a trailer out there, don't listen to her; she's on a crazy mean drunk, out to make trouble for a capable doctor who's been called by someone out there, an emergency call. So I thought I'd warn you, thank you. [MONK hangs up the telephone.]

[VIOLET comes downstage, and the light is focused on her.]

VIOLET: It's perfectly true that I have a room over the amusement arcade facing the pier. But it wasn't like Leona describes it. It took me a while to get it in shipshape condition because I was not a well girl when I moved in there, but I got it clean and attractive. It wasn't luxurious but it was clean and attractive and had an atmosphere to it. I don't see anything wrong with living upstairs from the amusement arcade, facing the pier. I don't have a bath or a toilet but I keep myself clean with a sponge bath at the washbasin and use the toilet in the amusement arcade. Anyhow it was a temporary arrangement, that's all it was, a temporary arrangement . . .

[LEONA *returns to the bar.* BILL *rises quickly and walks over to the bar.*]

LEONA: One two, button my shoe, three, four, shut the door, five, six, pick up sticks . . . [*No one speaks.*] . . . Silence, absolute silence. Am I being ostracized? [*She goes to the table of* QUENTIN *and* BOBBY.] Well, boys, what went wrong?

QUENTIN: I'm afraid I don't know what you mean.

LEONA: Sure you know what I mean. You're not talking to each other, you don't even look at each other. There's some kind of tension between you. What is it? Is it guilt feelings? Embarrassment with guilt feelings?

BOBBY: I still don't know what you mean, but, uh . . .

LEONA: 'But, uh' what?

QUENTIN: Don't you think you're being a little presumptuous?

LEONA: Naw, I know the gay scene. I learned it from my kid brother. He came out early, younger than this boy here. I know the gay scene and I know the language of it and I know how full it is of sickness and sadness; it's so full of sadness and sickness, I could almost be glad that my little brother died before he had time to be infected with all that sadness and sickness in the heart of a gay boy. This kid from Iowa, here, reminds me a little of how my brother was, and you, you remind me of how he might have become if he'd lived.

QUENTIN: Yes, you should be relieved he's dead, then.

[*She flops awkwardly into a chair at the table.*]

QUENTIN [*testily*]: Excuse me, won't you sit down?

LEONA: D'ya think I'm still standing up?

QUENTIN: Perhaps we took your table.

LEONA: I don't have any table. I'm moving about tonight like an animal in a zoo because tonight is the night of the death-day of my brother and . . . Look, the barman won't serve me, he thinks I'm on a mean drunk, so do me a favour, order a double bourbon and pretend it's for you. Do that, I'll love you for it, and of course I'll pay you for it.

QUENTIN [*calling out*]: Barman? I'd like a double bourbon.

MONK: If it's for the lady, I can't serve you.

[BILL *laughs heartily at the next table.*]

QUENTIN: It isn't for the lady, it's for me.

LEONA: How do you like that shit? [*She shrugs.*] Now what went wrong between you before you come in here, you can tell me and maybe I can advise you. I'm practically what they call a faggot's moll.

QUENTIN: Oh. Are you?

LEONA: Yes, I am. I always locate at least one gay bar in whatever city I'm in. I live in a home on wheels, I live in a trailer, so I been quite a few places. And have a few more to go. Now nobody's listening to us, they're involved in their own situations. What went wrong?

QUENTIN: Nothing, exactly. I just made a mistake, and he did, too.

LEONA: Oh. Mistakes. How did you make these mistakes? Nobody's listening, tell me.

QUENTIN: I passed him riding his bicycle up Canyon Road and I stopped my car and reversed it till I was right by his bike and I . . . spoke to him.

LEONA: What did you say to him?

BOBBY: Do you have to talk about it?

QUENTIN: Why not? I said: 'Did you really ride that bike all the way from Iowa to the Pacific Coast?' and he grinned and said, yes, he'd done that. And I said: 'You must be tired?' and he said he was and I said: 'Put your bike in the back seat of my car and come home with me for dinner.'

LEONA: What went wrong? At dinner? You didn't *give* him the dinner?

QUENTIN: No, I gave him drinks, first, because I thought that after he'd had dinner, he might say: 'Thank you, good night.'

BOBBY: Let's shut up about that. I had dinner after.

LEONA: After what?

QUENTIN: After . . .

BOBBY: I guess to you people who live here it's just an old thing you're used to, I mean the ocean out there, the Pacific, it's not an *experience* to you any more like it is to me. You say it's the Pacific, but me, I say THE PACIFIC!

QUENTIN: Well, everything is in 'caps' at your age, Bobby.

LEONA [*to* QUENTIN]: Do you work for the movies?

QUENTIN: Naturally, what else?

LEONA: Act in them, you're an actor?

QUENTIN: No. Script writer.

LEONA [*vaguely*]: Aw, you write movies, huh?

QUENTIN: Mostly rewrite. Adapt. Oh, I had a bit of a setback when they found me too literate for my first assignment . . . converting an epic into a vehicle for the producer's doxy, a grammar school dropout. But the industry is using me now to make blue movies bluer with . . . you know, touches of special . . . erotica . . . lovely.

[LEONA *laughs.*]

LEONA: Name?

QUENTIN: Quentin . . . Miss? [*He rises.*]

LEONA: Leona. Dawson. And he's?

QUENTIN: Bobby.

LEONA: Bobby, come back to the party. I want you back here, love. Resume your seat. [*Resting a hand on the boy's stiff shoulder*] . . . You're a literary gent with the suede shit-kickers and a brass-button blazer and a . . . [*Flicks his scarf.*]

BILL [*leering from bar*]: Ask him if he's got change for a three-dollar bill.

QUENTIN: Yes, if you have the bill.

LEONA: Ignore the peasants. I don't think that monkey-faced mother will serve us that bourbon . . . I never left his bar without leaving a dollar tip on the table, and this is what thanks I get for it, just because it's the death-day of my brother and I showed a little human emotion about it. Now what's the trouble between you and this kid from Iowa where the tall corn blows, I mean grows?

QUENTIN: I only go for straight trade. But this boy . . . look at him! Would you guess he was gay? . . . I didn't, I thought he was straight. But I had an unpleasant surprise when he responded to my hand on his knee by putting his hand on mine.

BOBBY: I don't dig the word 'gay'. To me they mean nothing, those words.

LEONA: Aw, you've got plenty of time to learn the meanings of words and cynical attitudes. Why he's got eyes like my brother's! Have you paid him?

QUENTIN: For disappointment?

LEONA: Don't be a mean-minded mother. Give him a five, a ten. If you picked up what you don't want, it's your mistake and pay for it.

BOBBY: I don't want money from him. I thought he was nice, I liked him.

LEONA: Your mistake, too [*She turns to* QUENTIN.] Gimme your wallet.

[QUENTIN *hands her his wallet.*]

BOBBY: He's disappointed. I don't want anything from him.

LEONA: Don't be a fool. Fools aren't respected, you fool. [*She removes a bill from the wallet and stuffs it in the pocket of* BOBBY's *shirt.* BOBBY *starts to return it.*] OK, I'll hold it for you till he cuts out of here to make another pickup and remind me to give it back to you when he goes. He wants to pay you, it's part of his sad routine. It's like doing penance . . . penitence.

BILL [*loudly*]: Monk, where's the head?

MONK: None of that here, Bill.

QUENTIN [*with a twist of a smile towards* BILL]: Pity.

LEONA [*turning to* QUENTIN]: Do you like being alone except for vicious pickups? The kind you go for? If I understood you correctly? . . . Christ, you have terrible eyes, the expression in them! What are you looking at?

QUENTIN: The fish over the bar . . .

LEONA: You're changing the subject.

QUENTIN: No, I'm not, not a bit . . . Now suppose some night I woke up and I found that fantastic fish . . . what is it?

LEONA: Sailfish. What about it?

QUENTIN: Suppose I woke up some midnight and found that peculiar thing swimming around in my bedroom? Up the Canyon?

LEONA: In a fish bowl? Aquarium?

QUENTIN: No, not in a bowl or aquarium: free, unconfined.

LEONA: Impossible.

QUENTIN: Granted. It's impossible. But suppose it occurred just the same, as so many impossible things *do* occur just the same. Suppose I woke up and discovered it there, swimming round and round in the darkness over my bed, with a faint phosphorescent glow in its big goggle-eyes and its gorgeously iridescent fins and tail making a swishing sound as it circles around and around and about right over my head in my bed.

LEONA: Hah!

QUENTIN: Now suppose this admittedly preposterous thing did occur. What do you think I would say?

LEONA: To the fish?

QUENTIN: To myself and the fish.

LEONA: . . . I'll be raped by an ape if I can imagine what a person would say in a situation like that.

QUENTIN: I'll tell you what I would say, I would say: 'Oh, well . . .'

LEONA: . . . Just 'Oh, well'?

QUENTIN: 'Oh, well' is all I would say before I went back to sleep.

LEONA: What I would say is: 'Get the hell out of here, you goggle-eyed monstrosity of a mother,' that's what I'd say to it.

MONK: Leona, let's lighten it up.

QUENTIN: You don't see the point of my story?

LEONA: Nope.

QUENTIN [*to* BOBBY]: Do *you* see the point of my story?

[BOBBY *shakes his head.*]

Well, maybe I don't either.

LEONA: Then why'd you tell it?

QUENTIN: What is the thing that you mustn't lose in this world

before you're ready to leave it? The one thing you mustn't lose
ever?

LEONA: . . . Love?

[QUENTIN *laughs*.]

BOBBY: Interest?

QUENTIN: That's closer, much closer. Yes, that's almost it. The word
that I had in mind is surprise, though. The capacity for being surprised. I've lost the capacity for being surprised, so completely
lost it, that if I woke up in my bedroom late some night and saw
that fantastic fish swimming right over my head, I wouldn't be
really surprised.

LEONA: You mean you'd think you were dreaming?

QUENTIN: Oh, no. Wide awake. But not really surprised. [*The special
spot concentrates on him. The bar dims, but an eerie glow should remain
on the sailfish over the bar.*] There's a coarseness, a deadening
coarseness, in the experience of most homosexuals. The experiences are quick, and hard, and brutal, and the pattern of them is
practically unchanging. Their act of love is like the jabbing of a
hypodermic needle to which they're addicted but which is more
and more empty of real interest and surprise. This lack of variation and surprise in their . . . 'love life' . . . [*He smiles harshly*] . . .
spreads into other areas of . . . 'sensibility?' [*He smiles again.*] . . .
Yes, once, quite a long while ago, I was often startled by the sense
of being alive, of being *myself*, *living*! Present on earth, in the
flesh, yes, for some completely mysterious reason, a single, separate, intensely conscious being, *myself*: *living*! . . . Whenever I
would feel this . . . *feeling*, this . . . shock of . . . what? . . . self-
realization? . . . I would be stunned, I would be thunderstruck by
it. And by the existence of everything that exists, I'd be lightning-
struck with astonishment . . . it would do more than astound me,
it would give me a feeling of panic, the sudden sense of . . . I suppose it was like an epileptic seizure, except that I didn't fall to the
ground in convulsions; no, I'd be more apt to try to lose myself
in a crowd on a street until the seizure was finished . . . They

were dangerous seizures. One time I drove into the mountains and smashed the car into a tree, and I'm not sure if I *meant* to do that, or . . . In a forest you'll sometimes see a giant tree, several hundred years old, that's scarred, that's blazed by lightning, and the wound is almost obscured by the obstinately still living and growing bark. I wonder if such a tree has learned the same lesson that I have, not to feel astonishment any more but just go on, continue for two or three hundred years more? . . . This boy I picked up tonight, the kid from the tall corn country, still has the capacity for being surprised by what he sees, hears and feels in this kingdom of earth. All the way up the canyon to my place, he kept saying, *I can't believe it, I'm here, I've come to the Pacific, the world's greatest ocean!* . . . as if nobody, Magellan or Balboa or even the Indians had ever seen it before him; yes, like he'd discovered this ocean, the largest on earth, and so now, because he'd found it himself, it existed, now, for the first time, never before . . . And this excitement of his reminded me of my having lost the ability to say: 'My God!' instead of just: 'Oh, well.' I've asked all the questions, shouted them at deaf heaven, till I was hoarse in the voice box and blue in the face, and gotten no answer, not the whisper of one, nothing at all, you see, but the sun coming up each morning and going down that night, and the galaxies of the night sky trooping onstage like chorines, robot chorines: one, two, three, kick, one two, three, kick . . . Repeat any question too often and what do you get, what's given? . . . A big carved rock by the desert, a . . . monumental symbol of worn-out passion and bewilderment in you, a stupid stone paralysed sphinx that knows no answers that you don't but comes on like the oracle of all time, waiting on her belly to give out some outcries of universal wisdom, and if she woke up some midnight at the edge of the desert and saw that fantastic fish swimming over her head . . . y'know what she'd say, too? She'd say: 'Oh, well' . . . and go back to sleep for another five thousand years. [*He turns back; and the bar is relighted. He returns to the table and adjusts his neckscarf as he speaks to* BOBBY.] . . . Your bicycle's still in my car. Shall I put it on the sidewalk?

BOBBY: I'll go get it.

QUENTIN: No. You will find it here, by the door. [*Desires no further exposure to* BOBBY.]

LEONA [*to* BOBBY]: Stay here awhile ... Set down. He wants to escape.

BOBBY: From me? [*Meaning 'Why?'*]

LEONA [*visibly enchanted by* BOBBY, *whom she associates with her lost brother*]: Maybe more from himself. Stay here awhile.

BOBBY: ... It's ... late for the road. [*But he may resume his seat here.*]

LEONA: On a bike, yeh, too late, with the dreaded fog people out. Y'know, I got a suggestion. It's sudden but it's terrific. [*She leans across the table, urgently.*] Put your bike in my trailer. It's got two bunks.

BOBBY: Thank you but ...

LEONA: It wouldn't cost you nothing and we'd be company for each other. My trailer's not ordinary, it's a Fonda deluxe, stereo with two speakers, colour TV with an eight-inch screen, touchamatic, and baby, you don't look well fed. I'm a hell of a cook, could qualify as a pro in that line, too.

BILL [*to* STEVE]: What a desperate pitch. I was the wrong sex. She wants a fruit in her stinkin' trailer.

LEONA: Nothing stunk in my trailer but what's out now ... He can't understand a person wanting to give protection to another, it's past his little reception. [*To* BOBBY] Why're you staring out into space with visibility zero?

BOBBY [*slowly, with a growing ardour*]: I've got a lot of important things to think over alone, new things. I feel new vibes, vibrations, I've got to sort out alone.

LEONA: Mexico's a dangerous country for you, and there's lonely stretches of road ... [*She's thinking of herself, too.*]

BOBBY: [*firmly but warmly to her*]: Yes ... I need that, now.

LEONA: Baby, are you scared I'd put the make on you?

[BILL *grunts contemptuously but with the knowledge that he is now truly evicted.*]

I don't, like they say, come on heavy ... never, not with ... [*She lightly touches* BOBBY's *hand on the table.*] This is my touch! Is it *heavy*?

[BOBBY *rises.* QUENTIN *is seen dimly, setting the bicycle at the door.*]

BOBBY: That man didn't come on heavy. [*Looking out at* QUENTIN.] His hand on my knee was just a human touch and it seemed natural to me to return it.

LEONA: Baby, his hand had … ambitions … And, oh, my God, you've got the skin and hair of my brother and even almost the eyes!

BILL: Can he play the fiddle?

BOBBY: In Goldenfield, Iowa, there was a man like that, ran a flower shop with a back room, decorated Chinese, with incense and naked pictures, which he invited boys into. I heard about it. Well, things like that aren't tolerated for long in towns like Goldenfield. There's suspicion and talk and then public outrage and action, and he had to leave so quick he didn't clear out the shop. [*The bar lights have faded out, and the special spot illuminates* BOBBY.] A bunch of us entered one night. The drying-up flowers rattled in the wind and the windchimes tinkled and the … naked pictures were just … pathetic, y'know. Except for a sketch of Michelangelo's David. I don't think anyone noticed me snatch it off the wall and stuff it into my pocket. Dreams … images … nights … On the plains of Nebraska I passed a night with a group of runaway kids my age and it got cold after sunset. A lovely wild young girl invited me under a blanket with just a smile, and then a boy, me between, and both of them kept saying 'love', one of 'em in one ear and one in the other, till I didn't know which was which 'love' in which ear or which … touch … The plain was high and the night air … exhilarating and the touches not heavy … The man with the hangup has set my bike by the door. [*Extends his hand to* LEONA. *The bar is relighted.*] It's been a pleasure to meet a lady like you. Oh, I've got a lot of new adventures, experiences, to think over alone on my speed iron. I think I'll drive all night, I don't feel tired. [BOBBY *smiles as he opens the door and nods good-bye to Monk's Place.*]

LEONA: Hey, Iowa to Mexico, the money … here's the money!

[*She rushes to the door, but* BOBBY *is gone with his bicycle.*]

BILL: He don't want a lousy five bucks, he wants everything in the wallet. He'll roll the faggot and hop back on his bike looking sweet and innocent as her brother fiddling in church.

[LEONA *rushes out, calling.*]

STEVE: The Coast is overrun with 'em, they come running out here like animals out of a brushfire.

MONK [*as he goes to each table, collecting the empty cans and bottles, emptying ash trays on a large serving tray*]: I've got no moral objections to them as a part of humanity, but I don't encourage them here. One comes in, others follow. First thing you know you're operating what they call a gay bar and it sounds like a bird cage, they're standing three deep at the bar and lining up at the men's room. Business is terrific for a few months. Then in comes the law. The place is raided, the boys hauled off in the wagon, and your place is padlocked. And then a cop or gangster pays you a social visit, big smile, all buddy-buddy. You had a good thing going, a real swinging place, he tells you, but you needed protection. He offers you protection and you buy it. The place is reopened and business is terrific a few months more. And then? It's raided again, and the next time it's reopened, you pay out of your nose, your ears, and your ass. Who wants it? I don't want it. I want a small steady place that I can handle alone, that brings in a small, steady profit. No buddy-buddy association with gangsters and the police. I want to know the people that come in my place so well I can serve them their brand of liquor or beer before they name it, soon as they come in the door. And all their personal problems, I want to know that, too.

[VIOLET *begins to hum softly, swaying to and fro like a water plant. When* MONK *finishes cleaning off the tables, he returns behind the bar. The bar lights dim, and his special spot comes up.*]

I'm fond of, I've got an affection for, a sincere interest in my regular customers here. They send me post cards from wherever they go and tell me what's new in their lives and I am interested in it. Just last month one of them I hadn't seen in about five years, he died in Mexico City and I was notified of the death and that he'd willed me all he owned in the world, his personal effects and a two-hundred-fifty-dollar savings account in a bank. A thing like that is beautiful as music. These things, these people, take the place of a family in my life. I love to come down those steps from my room to open the place for the evening, and when I've closed for the night, I love climbing back up those steps with my can of Ballantine's ale, and the stories, the jokes, the confidences and confessions I've heard that night, it makes me feel not alone . . . I've had heart attacks, and I'd be a liar to say they didn't scare me and don't still scare me. I'll die some night up those steps, I'll die in the night alone, and I hope it don't wake me up, that I just slip away, quietly.

[LEONA *has returned. The light in the bar comes up but remains at a low level.*]

LEONA: . . . Is there a steam engine in here? Did somebody drive in here on a steam engine while I was out?

MONK [*returning from his meditation*]: . . . Did what?

LEONA: I hear something going huff-huff like an old locomotive pulling into a station. [*She is referring to a sound like a panting dog. It comes from* BILL *at the unlighted table where* VIOLET *is seated between him and* STEVE.] . . . Oh, well, my home is on wheels . . . Bourbon sweet, Monk.

MONK: Leona, you don't need another.

LEONA: Monk, it's after midnight, my brother's death-day is over, I'll be all right, don't worry. [*She goes to the bar.*] . . . It was selfish of me to wish he was still alive.

[*A pin-spot of light picks up* VIOLET's *tear-stained and tranced face at the otherwise dark table.*]

. . . She's got some form of religion in her hands . . .

CURTAIN

Act Two

An hour later. 'Group singing' is in progress at the table stage right. LEONA *is not participating. She is sitting moodily at the bar facing front.*

VIOLET: 'I don't want to set the world on fii-yuh.'

STEVE: 'I don't want to set the world on fii-yuh.'

VIOLET: I like old numbers best. Here's an oldie that I learned from my mother. [*She rises and assumes a sentimental look.*]

'Lay me where sweet flowers blos-som,

Where the dainty lily blows

Where the pinks and violets min-gle,

Lay me underneath the rose.'

LEONA: Shit. Y'don't need a rose to lay her, you could lay her under a cactus and she wouldn't notice the diff-rence.

[BILL *crosses to the bar for a beer.*]

I guess you don't think I'm serious about it, hitting the highway tonight.

[BILL *shrugs and crosses to a downstage table.*]

Well, I am, I'm serious about it. [*She sits at his table.*] An experienced expert beautician can always get work anywhere.

BILL: Your own appearance is a bad advertisement for your line of work.

LEONA: I don't care how I look as long as I'm clean and decent . . . and *self-supporting*. When I haul into a new town, I just look through the yellow pages of the telephone directory and pick out a beauty shop that's close to my trailer camp. I go to the shop and offer to work a couple of days for nothing, and after that couple of days I'm in like Flynn, and on my own terms, which is fifty per cent of charges for all I do, and my tips, of course, too. They like my work and they like my personality, my approach to customers. I keep them laughing.

BILL: You keep me laughing, too.

LEONA: ... Of course, there's things about you I'll remember with pleasure, such as waking up sometimes in the night and looking over the edge of the upper bunk to see you asleep in the lower. [BILL *leaves the table. She raises her voice to address the bar-at-large.*] Yeah, he slept in the lower 'cause when he'd passed out or nearly, it would of taken a derrick to haul him into the upper bunk. So I gave him the lower bunk and took the upper myself.

BILL: As if you never pass out. Is that the idea you're selling?

LEONA: When I pass out I wake up in a chair or on the floor, oh, no, the floor was good enough for me in your opinion, and some-times you stepped on me even, yeah, like I was a rug or a bug, because your nature is selfish. You think because you've lived off one woman after another woman after eight or ten women you're something superior, special. Well, you're special but not superior, baby. I'm going to worry about you after I've gone and I'm sure as hell leaving tonight, fog or no fog on the highway, but I'll worry about you because you refuse to grow up and that's a mistake that you make, because you can only refuse to grow up for a lim-ited period in your lifetime and get by with it ... I *loved* you! ... I'm not going to cry. It's only being so tired that makes me cry.

[VIOLET *starts weeping for her.*]

VIOLET: Bill, get up and tell Leona good-bye. She's a lonely girl with-out a soul in the world.

LEONA: I've got the world in the world, and McCorkle don't have to make the effort to get himself or any part of him up, it's easier to stay down. And as for being lonely, listen, ducks, that applies to every mother's son and daughter of us alive, we were given warn-ing of that before we were born almost, and yet ... When I come to a new place, it takes me two or three weeks, that's all it takes me, to find somebody to live with in my home on wheels and to find a night spot to hang out in. Those first two or three weeks are rough, sometimes I wish I'd stayed where I was before, but I know from experience that I'll find somebody and locate a night spot to booze in, and get acquainted with . . . friends . . . [*The light has focused on her. She moves downstage with her hands in her pockets, her face and voice very grave as if she were less confident that things will be as she says.*] And then, all at once, something wonderful happens. All the past disappointments in people I left behind me, just disappear, evaporate from my mind, and I just remember the good things, such as their sleeping faces, and . . . Life! Life! I never just said, 'Oh, well,' I've always said 'Life!' to life, like a song to God, too, because I've lived in my lifetime and not been afraid of . . . changes . . . [*She goes back to the bar.*] . . . However, y'see, I've got this pride in my nature. When I live with a person I love and care for in my life, I expect his respect, and when I see I've lost it, I GO, GO! . . . So a home on wheels is the only right home for me.

[VIOLET *starts towards* LEONA.]

What is she doing here?

[VIOLET *has weaved to the bar.*]

Hey! What are *you* doing here?

VIOLET: You're the best friend I ever had, the best friend I . . . [*She sways and sobs like a* religieuse *in the grip of a vision.*]

LEONA: What's that, what're you saying?

[VIOLET *sobs.*]

She can't talk. What was she saying?

VIOLET: . . . BEST . . . !

LEONA: WHAT?

VIOLET: . . . *Friend!*

LEONA: I'd go further than that, I'd be willing to bet I'm the *only* friend that you've had, and the next time you come down sick nobody will bring you nothing, no chicken, no hot beef bouillon, no chinaware, no silver, and no interest and concern about your condition, and you'll die in your rattrap with no human voice, just bang, bang, bang from the bowling alley and billiards. And when you die you should feel a relief from the conditions you lived in. Now I'm leaving you two suffering, bleeding hearts together, I'm going to sit at the bar. I had a Italian boy friend that taught me saying, '*Meglior solo que mal accompagnato*', which means that you're better alone than in the company of a bad companion.

[*She starts to the bar, as* DOC *enters.*]

Back already, huh? It didn't take you much time to deliver the baby. Or did you bury the baby? Or did you bury the mother? Or did you bury them both, the mother and baby?

DOC [*to* MONK]: Can you shut up this woman?

LEONA: Nobody can shut up this woman. Quack, quack, quack, Doctor Duck, quack, quack, quack, quack, quack!

DOC: I'M A LICENSED PHYSICIAN!

LEONA: SHOW *me your licence. I'll shut up when I see it!*

DOC: A doctor's licence to practise isn't the size of a drunken driver's licence you put in a wallet, you hang it on the wall of your office.

LEONA: Here is your office! Which wall is your licence hung on? Beside the sailfish or where? Where is your licence to practise hung up, in the gents', with other filthy scribbles?!

MONK: Leona, you said your brother's death-day was over and I thought you meant you were . . .

LEONA: THOUGHT I MEANT I WAS *WHAT*?

MONK: You were ready to cool it. BILL! . . . Take Leona home, now.

LEONA: Christ, do you think I'd let him come near me?! Or near my trailer?! Tonight?! [*She slaps the bar several times with her sailor cap, turning to the right and left as if toward off assailants, her great bosom heaving, a jungle-look in her eyes.*]

VIOLET: Steve, if we don't go now the King-burger stand will shut on us, and I've had nothing but liquids on my stomach all day. So I need a Whopper tonight.

[BILL *laughs.*]

STEVE: You'll get a hot dog with chili and everything on the way home. Get me . . . get me . . . get me. Grab and grope. You disgrace me! . . . your habits.

VIOLET: You're underdeveloped and you blame me.

LEONA [*looking out*]: Yes . . . [*She slaps something with her cap.*] *Yes!*

VIOLET: What did she mean by that? Another sarcastic crack?

LEONA: When I say 'yes' it is not sarcastic . . . It means a decision to act.

MONK: The place is closing so will everybody get themselves together now, please.

VIOLET: I do have to have something solid. Too much liquids and not enough solids in the system upsets the whole system. Ask the Doc if it don't. Doc, don't it upset the system, liquids without solids? All day long?

> [DOC *has been sunk in profoundly dark and private reflections. He emerges momentarily to reply to* VIOLET's *direct question.*]

DOC: If that's a professional question to a doctor whose office is here . . . [*A certain ferocity is boiling in him and directed mostly at himself.*] My fee is . . . another brandy. [*He turns away with a short, disgusted laugh.*]

MONK: Something wrong, Doc?

> [VIOLET *has crossed to* BILL, *as a child seeking protection.*]

DOC: Why, no, what could be wrong? But a need to put more liquid in my system . . .

LEONA [*convulsively turning about*]: Yes . . . yes! [*This no longer relates to anything but her private decision.*]

BILL [*to himself*]: I'm not about to spend the night on the beach . . .

VIOLET: [*leaning towards* BILL]: I am not neither, so why don't we check in somewhere? Us, two, together?

STEVE: I heard that.

LEONA: Yes . . . *yes!*

MONK: I said the place is closing.

VIOLET: Let's go together, us three, and talk things over at the Kingburger stand.

STEVE: Being a cook I know the quality of those giant hamburgers called Whoppers, and they're fit only for dog food.

VIOLET: I think we better leave, now. [*Extends her delicate hands to both men.*] Steve? Bill? [*They all rise unsteadily and prepare to leave.*] Bill, you know I feel so protected now. [VIOLET, STEVE, *and* BILL *start out.*]

LEONA [*stomping the floor with a powerful foot*]: Y' WANT YOUR ASS IN A SLING BEFORE YOU'RE LAID UNDER THAT ROSE?

VIOLET [*shepherded past* LEONA *by* STEVE *and* BILL]: If we don't see you again, good luck wherever you're going.

[*They go out to the door.*]

LEONA [*rushing after them*]: That's what she wants, she wants her ass in a sling!

[*She rushes out the door. A moment or two later, as* MONK *looks out, and above the boom of the surf,* VIOLET's *histrionically shrill out-cries are heard. This is followed by an off-stage quarrel between* LEONA *and a night watchman on the beach. Their overlapping, ad-lib dialogue continues in varying intensity as background to the business on stage: 'If you don't settle down and come along peaceful-like, I'm going to call the wagon! . . .' 'Do that, I just dare you to do it – go on, I just dare you to call the wagon! I want to ride in a wagon – it's got wheels, hasn't it – I'll ride any Goddam thing on wheels! . . .' 'Oh, no – listen, lady, what's your name anyhow? . . .' 'I'm just the one to do it! . . . I tell you my name? I'm going to tell you my name? What's your name? I want your name! Oh boy, do I want your name! . . .' 'Listen, please, come on, now, let's take this thing easy . . .' 'I've been drinking in this bar, and it's not the first time you . . .' 'Let's go! You raise hell every night! . . .' 'Every night! This isn't the first time – I've been meaning to report you! Yes, I'm going to report you! Yes, how's that for a switch? . . .' 'I'm just trying to do my duty! . . .' 'I live in a home on wheels, and every night you try to molest me when I come home! . . .' 'No! You're wrong – you're always in there drinking and raising hell and . . .' 'Yeah, but you let criminals go free, right? . . .' 'No, I don't! . . .' 'People can't walk in*] the street, murdering, robbing, thieving, and all I do is have a few Goddam drinks, just because it's my brother's death-day, so I was showing a little human emotion – take your hands off me! . . .' 'Come on now! . . .' 'Don't you put your hands on a lady like me! . . .' 'No, I'm not! . . .' 'I'm a Goddam lady! That's what I am, and you just lay off! . . .' 'I've had enough of this! . . .' 'Every night I come out here, you're looking for free drinks, that's what's the matter with you! . . .' 'I've never had a drink in my life, lady! . . .' 'You never had a drink in your life! . . .' 'No, I haven't, I've . . .' 'Show me your identification, that's what I want to see! . . .' 'I'm just trying to do my duty . . .' 'Look here, old man . . .' 'I don't know why I have to put up with an old dame like you this way . . .' 'Oh! – Oh! – Why you Goddam son of a! . . .' 'Now! . . .' 'Don't you talk to me like that . . .' 'I'm not talking to you, I'm telling you to come over here and let me get you to the telephone here! . . .' 'You've been harassing that man Monk! . . .' 'I'm not harassing anybody! . . .' 'You're not harassing anybody? . . .' 'You come over to this Monk's Place every night and raise hell, the whole damn bunch of you, and a poor man like me trying to earn a few dollars and make a living for his old woman and . . .' 'Let me see your identification! What precinct are you from? . . .' 'Oh, yeah . . .' 'Go on, I want that identification, and I want that uniform off you, and that badge . . .' 'You won't do anything of the sort! . . .' 'Oh, yeah . . .' 'Yes, I'm doing my job, what I'm doing is legal! . . .' 'I happen to have more influence up at that station than you . . . Goddam pig! . . .' 'I haven't done nothing to you, I'm just trying to do my job . . .' 'Do your job? . . .' 'Yes, and you're giving me a lot of hard time! . . .' 'There's raping and thieving and criminals and robbers walking the streets, breaking store fronts, breaking into every bar . . .' 'Well, that's not my – listen, lady! I'm just the night watch-man around this beach here. I'm just on the beach nights, I don't have anything to do with what's going on somewhere else in the city, just on this beach! . . .' 'You don't know what's going on on the beach . . .' 'I know what's going on on the beach, and it's you and that crowd drinking every night, raising hell! . . .' 'We're not raising hell every night! . . .' 'If I was your husband, golly, I – I – by God I would take care of you, I wouldn't put up with your likes, you and that crowd drinking every night! . . .' 'I like that uniform you've got on you, and I'm gonna have it! . . .' 'Why do you have to pick on a little man like me for? . . .' 'I've seen you sneaking around, Peeping Tom, that's what you are! . . .' 'No, that's not so! . . .' 'I've seen you sneaking around looking in ladies' windows . . .' 'That's not true! I'm just trying to do my duty! I keep telling you . . .' 'Yeah, peeping in windows . . .' 'No! . . .' 'Watching people undress . . .' 'No! You . . .' 'I've seen you, you lascivious old man! . . .' 'I've seen you taking these young men over to your trailer court and making studs out of them! . . .' 'Yeah! – Yeah! – Yeah! – Men, that's what I take to my trailer! I wouldn't take a palsied old man like you! . . .' 'You know damn well I wasn't trying to get you to . . . ! I was trying to get you to this telephone box, where I was going to! . . .' 'You will not be able to, old man! . . .' 'Listen, Miss, I asked you to give me your identification! You give me your identification so I can tell who you are! . . .' 'I want your identification! I've seen you, I've seen you sneaking around the trailer court, I've seen you looking in windows . . .' 'Oh, that's a lie! I never did a thing like that in all my life, I go to church. I'm a good Christian man! . . .' 'Oh yeah! Yeah! Yeah! . . .' 'I could take you in if I were younger, I wouldn't have to call the highway patrol, but I'm going to do that right now! . . .' 'Listen, Holy Willie! I've seen your likes in church before! I wouldn't trust you with a . . .' 'A little church wouldn't do you any harm neither! . . .' 'Old man . . . Yeah! Yeah! . . .' 'I've seen you with those young studs! . . .' 'Doesn't that make you excited? . . .' 'No, by God, it doesn't! . . .' 'Is that your problem? . . .' 'No, I don't have none! You're the one with the hang-ups and problems – you are a problem! You hang out here all night in that damn Monk's Place! . . .' 'I've got my own man, I don't have to worry about any other man, I got my own man in my trailer! . . .' 'Anyone want to spend the night with you, he must be a pig then, he must be some kind of pig living with you! . . .' 'Fat old bag of wind, don't you talk to me! . . .' 'Look, I'm tired of talking to you, by God, I've put up with you all I'm going to! I told you I was going to call the highway patrol! . . .' 'I've seen the way you look at me when you . . .' 'That's a lie! – I never . . .' 'Yeah! Yeah! . . .' 'I – I . . .' 'I've seen you skulking around in the *dark, looking in windows! . . .' 'I don't need your kind! I've got a good woman at home, and she takes care of me, she takes good care of me! If I can get this job done and you'll just settle down and be quiet, we wouldn't have all this noise! . . .' 'Does your wife know about the girls you go out with? . . .' 'You're trying to incriminate me! . . .' 'Does she know about that? . . .' 'I know what you're trying to do . . .' 'I've seen you . . .' 'Trying to get me in trouble! Trying to get me to lose my job here! . . .' 'I know what you holy boys are like! . . .' 'Why don't you go back in there and raise some more hell with those young studs? . . .' 'I ain't doing that neither . . .' 'If you'd be quiet! . . .' 'Stop harassing! . . .' 'I ain't harassing nothing! . . .' 'Every time you want a drink, yes? . . .' 'I don't, I don't . . .'*]

MONK [*to* DOC]: Goddam, she's left her suitcase.

DOC [*musing darkly*]: . . . Done what?

MONK: She's left that bag in here, which means she's coming back.

DOC: Aw, yeah, a guarantee of it, she's going to provide you with the solace of her companionship up those stairs to the living quarters. [*He faces out from the bar.*] Y'know, that narrow flight of stairs is like the uterine passage to life, and I'd say that strange, that amorphous-looking creature is expecting to enter the world up the uterine passage to your living quarters above. [*He rises, chuckling darkly.*] Is the toilet repaired in the gents' room?

MONK [*listening to noises outside*]: Yeh, plumber fixed it today.

[DOC *sighs and lumbers heavily the way pointed by the chalk-white hand signed 'GENTS' off stage right.*

MONK *crosses to the door to assess the disturbance outside.* BILL *rushes into the bar.*]

BILL: For Chrissake, get an ambulance with a strait jacket for her.

MONK: You mean you can't hold her, you stupid prick?

BILL: No man can hold that woman when she goes ape. Gimme a dime, I'm gonna call the Star of the Sea psycho ward.

MONK: Don't put a hand on that phone.

[VIOLET *now rushes in the door. She continues her histrionic outcries.*]

VIOLET: They're callin' the wagon for her, she's like a wild thing out there, lock the door, don't let her at me. Hide me, help me! Please!

[*She rushes towards the stairs.*]

MONK: Stay down those stairs, pick up your luggage, I'll . . . I'll . . . call a taxi for you.

VIOLET: Steve done nothin' to . . . nothin' . . . Just run!

[*Altercation rises outside.* VIOLET *rushes into the ladies'.* MONK *closes the door and bolts it.* DOC *returns from the gents', putting on his jacket. His pant cuffs are wet.*]

DOC: The toilet still overflows.

[STEVE *calls at the locked door.*]

STEVE: Vi'let? Monk?

[MONK *admits him.* STEVE *enters with a confused look about, two dripping hot dogs in his hand.*]

STEVE: Vi'let, is Vi'let, did Vi'let get back in here?

MONK: Yeh, she's back in the ladies'. [MONK *closes door.*]

STEVE [*shuffling rapidly to the ladies'*]: Vi'let? Vi'let? Hear me?

MONK: No. She don't.

STEVE: Vi'let, the King-burger's closed. So I couldn't get a Whopper . . . I got you two dogs, with chili and sauerkraut. You can come out now, Leona's getting arrested. Violet screamed for help to a cop that hates and hassles me ev'ry time I go home.

MONK: Those dogs you're holding are dripping on the floor.

DOC: Committing a nuisance . . .

STEVE: Vi'let, the dogs'll turn cold, the chili's dripping off 'em. You can't stay all night in a toilet, Vi'let.

VIOLET [*from the ladies'*]: I can, I will, go away.

STEVE: She says she's gonna stay all night in a toilet. Wow . . . I mean . . .wow. [*Starts eating one of the hot dogs with a slurping sound.*]

MONK: If she's called the law here I want her to shut up in there.

STEVE: Vi'let, shut up in there. Come out for your dog.

VIOLET: Take your dog away and leave me alone. You give me no protection and no support a'tall.

[DOC *utters a laugh that is dark with an ultimate recognition of human absurdity and his own self-loathing.*]

MONK [*touching his chest*]: . . . Doc? . . . Have a nightcap with me.

DOC: Thanks, Monk, I could use one.

MONK [*leaning back in chair and tapping his upper abdomen*]: Angina or gastritis, prob'ly both.

DOC: In that location, it's gas.

MONK: What happened at Treasure Island?

DOC [*sipping his 'shot'*]: Tell you when I . . . get this . . . down.

BILL: Time . . . runs out with one and you go to another. Got a call from a woman guv'ment employee in Sacramento. She's got a co-op in a high-rise condominium, lives so high on the hog with payoffs an' all she can't see ground beneath her.

MONK: Why're you shouting, at who?

BILL: Nobody's ever thrown McCorkle out.

MONK: Unusual and not expected things can happen.

[LEONA *is heard from off stage:* '*Okay, you make your phone call, and I'll make mine.*']

So, Doc, how'd it go at the trailer camp?

[*He and* DOC *are seated in profile at the downstage table.* STEVE *and* BILL *are silhouetted at the edge of the lighted area.*]

DOC: The birth of the baby was at least three months premature, so it was born dead, of course, and just beginning to look like a human baby . . . The man living with the woman in the trailer said, 'Don't let her see it, get it out of the trailer.' I agreed with the man that she shouldn't see it, so I put this foetus in a shoe box . . . [*He speaks with difficulty, as if compelled to.*] The trailer was right by the beach, the tide was coming in with heavy surf, so I put the shoe box . . . and contents . . . where the tide would take it.

MONK: . . . Are you sure that was legal?

DOC: Christ, no, it wasn't legal . . . I'd barely set the box down when the man came out shouting for me. The woman had started to haemorrhage. When I went back in the trailer, she was bleeding to death. The man hollered at me, 'Do something, can't you do something for her!'

MONK: . . . Could you?

DOC: . . . I could have told the man to call an ambulance for her, but I thought of the probable consequences to me, and while I thought about that, the woman died. She was a small woman, but not small enough to fit in a shoe box, so I . . . I gave the man a fifty-dollar bill that I'd received today for performing an abortion. I gave it to him in return for his promise not to remember my name . . . [*He reaches for the bottle. His hand shakes so that he can't refill his shot-glass.* MONK *fills it for him.*] . . . You see, I can't make out certificates of death, since I have no legal right any more to practise medicine, Monk.

MONK: . . . In the light of what happened, there's something I'd better tell you, Doc. Soon as you left here to deliver that baby, Leona ran out of the bar to make a phone call to the office at Treasure Island, warning them that you were on your way out there to deliver a baby. So, Doc, you may be in trouble . . . If you stay here . . .

DOC: I'll take a Benzedrine tablet and pack and . . .

MONK: Hit the road before morning.

DOC: I'll hit the road tonight.

MONK: Don't let it hit you. [*Stands to shake.*] G'bye, Doc. Keep in touch.

DOC: G'bye, Monk. Thanks for all and the warning.

MONK: Take care, Doc.

STEVE: Yeh, Doc, you got to take care. Bye, Doc.

BILL: No sweat, Doc, g'bye.

[DOC *exits.*]

MONK: That old son of a bitch's paid his dues . . .

[*Altercation rises outside once more: 'I'm gonna slap the cuffs on you! . . .' 'That does it, let go of me, you fink, you pig!' Approach of a squad car siren is heard at a distance.*]

Yep, coming the law!

BILL: I don't want in on this.

STEVE: Not me neither.

[*They rush out. Squad car screeches to a stop.* LEONA *appears at the door, shouting and pounding.*]

LEONA: MONK! THE PADDY WAGON IS SINGING MY SONG!

[MONK *lets her in and locks the door.*]

MONK: Go upstairs. Can you make it?

[*She clambers up the steps, slips, nearly falls.*

POLICEMAN *knocks at the door.* MONK *admits him.*]

Hi, Tony.

TONY: Hi, Monk. What's this about a fight going on here, Monk?

MONK: Fight? Not here. It's been very peaceful tonight. The bar is closed. I'm sitting here having a nightcap with . . .

TONY: Who's that bawling back there?

MONK [*pouring a drink for* TONY]: Some dame disappointed in love, the usual thing. Try this and if it suits you, take the bottle.

TONY [*He drinks.*]: . . . O.K. Good.

MONK: Take the bottle. Drop in more often. I miss you.

TONY: Thanks, g'night. [*He goes out.*]

MONK: Coast is clear, Leona. [*As* MONK *puts another bottle on the table,* LEONA *comes awkwardly back down the stairs.*]

LEONA: Monk? Thanks, Monk. [*She and* MONK *sit at the table.* VIOLET *comes out of the ladies' room.*]

VIOLET: Steve? . . . Bill? [*She sees* LEONA *at the table and starts to retreat.*]

LEONA: Aw, hell, Violet. Come over and sit down with us, we're having a nightcap, all of us, my brother's death-day is over.

VIOLET: Why does everyone hate me? [*She sits at the table: drinks are poured from the bottle.* VIOLET *hitches her chair close to* MONK'S. *In a few moments she will deliberately drop a matchbook under the table, bend to retrieve it, and the hand on* MONK*'s side will not return to the table surface.*]

LEONA: Nobody hates you, Violet. It would be a compliment to you if they did.

VIOLET: I'd hate to think that I'd come between you and Bill.

LEONA: Don't torture yourself with an awful thought like that. Two people living together is something you don't understand, and since you don't understand it you don't respect it, but, Violet, this being our last conversation, I want to advise something to you. I think you need medical help in the mental department and I think this because you remind me of a . . . of a . . . of a plant of some kind . . .

VIOLET: Because my name is Violet?

LEONA: No, I wasn't thinking of violets, I was thinking of water plants, yeah, plants that don't grow in the ground but float on water. With you everything is such a . . . such a . . . well, you know what I mean, don't you?

VIOLET: Temporary arrangement?

LEONA: Yes, you could put it that way. Do you know how you got into that place upstairs from the amusement arcade?

VIOLET: . . . How?

LEONA: Yes, *how* or *why* or *when*?

VIOLET: . . . Why, I . . . [*She obviously is uncertain on all three points.*]

LEONA: Take your time. And *think*. How, why, when?

VIOLET: Why, I was . . . in L.A., and . . .

LEONA: Are you sure you were in L.A.? Are you sure about even that? Or is everything foggy to you, is your mind in a cloud?

VIOLET: Yes, I was . . .

LEONA: I said take your time, don't push it. Can you come out of the fog?

MONK: Leona, take it easy, we all know Violet's got problems.

LEONA: Her problems are mental problems and I want her to face them, now, in our last conversation. Violet? Can you come out of the fog and tell us how, when, and why you're living out of a suitcase upstairs from the amusement arcade, can you just . . .

MONK [*cutting in*]: She's left the amusement arcade, she left it tonight, she came here with her suitcase.

LEONA: Yeah, she's a water plant, with roots in water, drifting the way it takes her.

[VIOLET *weeps*.]

And she cries too easy, the water works are back on. I'll give her some music to cry to before I go back to my home on wheels and get it cracking up the Old Spanish Trail. [*She rises from the table.*]

MONK: Not tonight, Leona. You have to sleep off your liquor before you get on the highway in this fog.

LEONA: That's what you think, not what I think, Monk. My time's run out in this place. [*She has walked to the juke box and started the violin piece.*] . . . How, when, and why, and her only answer is tears. Couldn't say how, couldn't say when, couldn't say why. And I don't think she's sure where she was before she come here, any more sure than she is where she'll go when she leaves here. She don't dare remember and she don't dare look forward, neither. Her mind floats on a cloud and her body floats on water. And her dirty fingernail hands reach out to hold on to something she hopes can hold her together. [*She starts back towards the table, stops; the bar dims and light is focused on her.*] . . . Oh, my God, she's at it again, she got a hand under the table. [LEONA *laughs sadly.*] Well, I guess she can't help it. It's sad, though. It's a pitiful thing to have to reach under a table to find some reason to live. You know, she's worshipping her idea of God Almighty in her personal church. Why the hell should I care she done it to a nowhere person that I put up in my trailer for a few months? I wish that kid from I-oh-a with eyes like my lost brother had been willing to travel with me, but I guess I scared him. What I think I'll do is turn back to a faggot's moll when I haul up to Sausalito or San Francisco. You always find one in the gay bars that needs a big sister with him, to camp with and laugh and cry with, and I hope I'll find one soon . . . it scares me to be alone in my home on wheels built for two . . . [*She turns as the bar is lighted and goes back to the table.*] Monk, HEY, MONK! What's my tab here t'night?

MONK: Forget it, don't think about it, go home and sleep, Leona. [*He and* VIOLET *appear to be in a state of trance together.*]

LEONA: I'm not going to sleep and I never leave debts behind me. This twenty ought to do it. [*She places a bill on the table.*]

MONK: Uh-huh, sure, keep in touch . . .

LEONA: Tell Bill he'll find his effects in the trailer-court office, and when he's hustled himself a new meal ticket, he'd better try and respect her, at least in public . . . Well . . . [*She extends her hand slightly.* MONK *and* VIOLET *are sitting with closed eyes.*] . . . I guess I've already gone.

VIOLET: G'bye, Leona.

MONK: G'bye . . .

LEONA: 'Meglior solo', huh, ducks? [LEONA *lets herself out of the bar.*]

MONK: . . . G'bye, Leona.

VIOLET: . . . Monk?

MONK. [*correctly suspecting her intent*]: You want your suitcase, it's . . .

VIOLET: I don't mean my suitcase, nothing valuable's in it but my . . . undies and . . .

MONK: Then what've you got in mind?

VIOLET: . . . In *what*?

MONK: Sorry. No offence meant. But there's taverns licensed for rooms, and taverns licensed for liquor and food and liquor, and I am a tavern only licensed for . . .

VIOLET [*overlapping with a tone and gesture of such ultimate supplication that it would break the heart of a stone*]: I just meant . . . let's go upstairs. Huh? Monk? [MONK *stares at her reflectively for a while, considering all the potential complications of her taking up semi- or permanent residence up there.*] Why're you looking at me that way? I just want a temporary, a night, a . . .

MONK: . . . Yeah, go on up and make yourself at home. Take a shower up there while I lock up the bar.

VIOLET: God love you, Monk, like me. [*She crosses, with a touch of 'labyrinthitis', to the stairs and mounts two steps.*] Monk! . . . I'm scared of these stairs, they're almost steep as a ladder. I better take off my slippers. Take my slippers off for me. [*There is a tone in her voice that implies she has already 'moved in' . . . She holds out one leg from the steps, then the other.* MONK *removes her slippers and she goes on up, calling down to him:*] Bring up some beer, sweetheart.

MONK: Yeh, I'll bring some beer up. Don't forget your shower. [*Alone in the bar,* MONK *crosses downstage.*] I'm going to stay down here till I hear that shower running, I am not going up there till she's took a shower. [*He sniffs the ratty slipper.*] Dirty, worn-out slipper still being worn, sour-smelling with sweat from being worn too long, but still set by the bed to be worn again the next day, walked on here and there on – pointless – errands till the sole's worn through, and even then not thrown away, just padded with cardboard till the cardboard's worn through and still not thrown away, still put on to walk on till it's . . . past all repair . . . [*He has been, during this, turning out lamps in the bar.*] Hey, Violet, will you for Chrissake take a . . . [*This shouted appeal breaks off with a disgusted laugh. He drops the slipper, then grins sadly.*] She probably thinks she'd dissolve in water. I shouldn't of let her stay here. Well, I won't touch her, I'll have no contact with her, maybe I won't even go up there tonight. [*He crosses to open the door. We hear the boom of the ocean outside.*] I always leave the door open for a few minutes to clear the smoke and liquor smell out of the place, the human odours, and to hear the ocean. Y'know, it sounds different this late than it does with the crowd on the beach-front. It has a private sound to it, a sound that's just for itself and for me. [MONK *switches off the blue neon sign. It goes dark outside. He closes door.*]

[*Sound of water running above. He slowly looks towards the sound.*]

That ain't rain.

[*Tired from the hectic night, maybe feeling a stitch of pain in his heart (but he's used to that),* MONK *starts to the stairs. In the spill of light beneath them, he glances up with a slow smile, wry, but not bitter. A smile that's old too early, but it grows a bit warmer as he starts up the stairs.*]

CURTAIN

PENGUIN MODERN CLASSICS

CAT ON A HOT TIN ROOF
TENNESSEE WILLIAMS

'One of the hottest, sultriest plays ever written' *Guardian*

'Big Daddy' Pollitt, the richest cotton planter in the Mississippi Delta, is about to celebrate his sixty-fifth birthday. His two sons have returned home for the occasion: Gooper, his wife and children, Brick, an ageing football hero who has turned to drink, and his feisty wife Maggie. As the hot summer evening unfolds, the veneer of happy family life and Southern gentility gradually slips away as unpleasant truths emerge and greed, lies, jealousy and suppressed sexuality threaten to reach boiling point. Made into a film starring Elizabeth Taylor and Paul Newman, *Cat on a Hot Tin Roof* is a masterly portrayal of family tensions and individuals trapped in prisons of their own making.

WINNER OF THE PULITZER PRIZE

PENGUIN MODERN CLASSICS

THE GLASS MENAGERIE
TENNESSEE WILLIAMS

'Tennessee Williams will live as long as drama itself' Peter Shaffer

Abandoned by her husband, Amanda Wingfield comforts herself with recollections of her earlier, more gracious life in Blue Mountain when she was pursued by 'gentleman callers'. Her son Tom, a poet with a job in a warehouse, longs for adventure and escape from his mother's suffocating embrace, while Laura, her shy crippled daughter, has her glass menagerie and her memories. Amanda is desperate to find her daughter a husband, but when the long-awaited gentleman caller does arrive, Laura's romantic illusions are crushed. *The Glass Menagerie*, Tennessee William's evocation of loneliness and lost love, is one of his most powerful and moving plays.

*Contemporary ... Provocative ... Outrageous ...
Prophetic ... Groundbreaking ... Funny ... Disturbing ...
Different ... Moving ... Revolutionary ... Inspiring ...
Subversive ... Life-changing ...*

What makes a modern classic?

At Penguin Classics our mission has always been to make the best
books ever written available to everyone. And that also means
constantly redefining and refreshing exactly what makes a 'classic'.
That's where Modern Classics come in. Since 1961 they have been an
organic, ever-growing and ever-evolving list of books from the last
hundred (or so) years that we believe will continue to be read over and
over again.

They could be books that have inspired political dissent, such as
Animal Farm. Some, like *Lolita* or *A Clockwork Orange*, may have
caused shock and outrage. Many have led to great films, from *In Cold
Blood* to *One Flew Over the Cuckoo's Nest*. They have broken down
barriers – whether social, sexual, or, in the case of *Ulysses*, the
boundaries of language itself. And they might – like *Goldfinger* or
Scoop – just be pure classic escapism. Whatever the reason, Penguin
Modern Classics continue to inspire, entertain and enlighten millions
of readers everywhere.

'No publisher has had more influence on reading habits than Penguin'
Independent

'Penguins provided a crash course in world literature'
Guardian

The best books ever written

PENGUIN 🐧 CLASSICS

SINCE 1946

Find out more at www.penguinclassics.com